him through me

making love and music in the Sixties & Seventies

a memoir

Pamela Windo

©2004-2014 Pamela Windo
All Rights Reserved

No part of this book may be reproduced in any form or by any electronic or mechanical means including information storage and retrieval systems without permission in writing from the publisher, except by a reviewer who may quote brief passages in a review.

Library of Congress Cataloging-in-Publication Data

Windo, Pamela, 1942- author.
him through me : making love and music in the Sixties and Seventies / a memoir by Pamela Windo.
pages cm
ISBN-13: 978-1497445376
1. Windo, Pamela, 1942- 2. Windo, Gary. 3. Punk rock musicians--Biography. 4. Jazz musicians--Biography. 5. Authors--Biography. I. Title.
2014

2014906868

To my sons, Simon and Jamie, and to Audrey Windo, for helping me remember....

ACKNOWLEDGMENTS

My thanks to all those who cheered me on as I found my way through the labyrinth of the various versions of this book: Ian Bennett; Michael King; Steve Feigenbaum; Judy Starger; Nick Mason; Sir Richard Branson; Robert Wyatt; Tobias Steed; Dan Hiscocks; Philip Dodd; Kevin Whitehead; Eleanor Lindsay-Fynn; Suzanne Murray; Martina Prior; Owen Keenan; Kathleen Wakefield; Sergio Amadori; John Ashton; Ian Kimmet; Knox Chandler; Ed Fitzgerald; Camille Romero; Keryn Sovella; Kendra Arnold; Hal Willner; Steve York, and special thanks to Dave Thompson.

Please forgive me if I have made any omissions. The same applies to photographs: I have used what I managed to hold onto over the years, and a few from here and there.

INTRODUCTION

I took on the task of writing an introduction with some misgivings—and that trepidation was justified. I had no idea that beneath that nice Mrs. Windo who lived down the road dwelt the kind of wild woman that we had been constantly warned about (and were constantly looking for). It's just a shame that I never realized it at the time; otherwise maybe I could have played a more major role in this book.

My life tracked alongside Pam and Gary's for a while in the seventies. They were good friends and great company; Gary's playing was an important step in my musical life, and the sessions at Britannia Row were great fun as well as productive—particularly so, as Gary's recordings were Britannia Row Studios' first project and something of a test session. We had designed the studio so we could operate on occasion without tape ops and engineers, and it worked. Animals was later recorded there, and probably most famously the kids of Islington Green School who supplied the choruses for "Another Brick in the Wall."

Pam and Gary introduced me to another world of music and musicians, and one that I still cherish. Many of those trick time signatures may have been beyond me, but many of the friendships sustain.

—Nick Mason, Pink Floyd

FOREWORD

"The only people for me are the mad ones, the ones who are mad to live, mad to talk, mad to be saved, desirous of everything at the same time, the ones who never yawn or say a commonplace thing, but burn, burn, burn like fabulous yellow roman candles exploding like spiders across the stars."
—Jack Kerouac, *On the Road*

That morning in July 1992, the heat was unbearably dry and working up to a sirocco. I'd walked over to the American Express bureau to see if there were any messages for me. The young man looked up and said, "Your sons called. You must call them."

I had gone to live in Morocco to get away from it all, to write a novel. There were as yet no mobile phones, and, where I lived, not even a land line. I was cut off, as I'd wanted to be. In the main post office, I gave the New York number to the operator. An hour later, I went into the phone booth.

"You'd better sit down," my elder son said, his voice distant and solemn over the transatlantic line. I could hear my younger son's agitated voice in the background. Someone close to me had died; I steeled myself to hear who it was and sank onto the booth's narrow bench.

"Gary died yesterday," he said, leaving a moment of terrible emptiness on the line. I felt the thud of shock followed by the sickening sense of inevitability: his prediction, that he wouldn't live a long life, rang in my ears. Had he simply decided it was his time?

He was just fifty years old. I'd known him since I was four, almost all my life. Just a few years before that call, I'd still been married to him: sixteen years on a journey that had bound us together, beyond anything either of us had ever imagined.

It was only later that I learned he'd come back from a tour in California with a rock 'n' roll band, business as usual; that he'd been suffering from a serious case of bronchial asthma, sicker than he'd cared to admit or than anyone knew.

When I left the post office, it was with a grim step. The sand- and dust-shrouded streets and violently swaying palm trees echoed the feelings of grief, guilt, and rage that had taken me over. I had fled to Morocco to gather myself back together; now I was demolished and would have to begin again.

◆

In later phone calls, I learned that the day after he was pronounced dead at the hospital my two sons—who were from my first marriage and had known him as their step-father since they were three and four—had gone to see with their own eyes where he'd died, and to retrieve whatever of his belongings they could find. After our divorce, he'd married an Irish Catholic girl half his age. When the glamour had worn off, she'd found a new boyfriend and had relegated Gary to the converted garage beneath her house.

It was my younger son who told me how he'd entered the garage room and had gone into a nauseous spin at the sight of the oxygen tank, and how he must have suffered, alone, at the end. I felt dizzy listening, recalling too vividly the frightening breathlessness of his asthma attacks: a memory that would never fade.

My son had looked around at the meager belongings, the shelf of LPs, and the beautiful Selmer saxophone which he placed in its black case—like a coffin. He came across some bags of heroin in a small pouch and flushed them down the toilet. My elder son gathered together the record albums and a few clothes. The little Chihuahua dog that had gone everywhere with him for the past few years was not there. Whatever cash he'd had, which he would always stash in the trunk of his car, along with bars of chocolate, had also vanished.

As I sheltered from the sandstorm in a nearby café, I remembered that a few weeks before his death, he had sent me a fax in care of a friend in Marrakech. It was handwritten, with a cartoon of his face, some chit-chat, and a row of xxxx's *To Carmus*, his special name for me. I hadn't seen any sign in it of what was about to happen and had written back, with chit-chat and xxxxs.

Back home, I pulled out the faded fax and as I re-read his words, a poem of Stevie Smith's came quickly to mind: "I was much further out than you thought. And not waving but drowning." I hadn't guessed he wasn't waving, and hadn't been there to prevent him drowning.

In the days after the call, an unexpected emptiness came over me, a sort of disbelief. I decided I would not go back to the United States. I was no longer his wife and from what I'd heard about his young widow, was clearly not welcome. And it would mean a costly flight for which I barely had funds, living as I was, out on a limb. By then, I'd lost touch with his friends and colleagues. His wife had provided no details of the funeral arrangements which I only later learned was a cremation; and nothing about what had happened at the end. The only thing she had said to my sons was: "We heard some shouting. We thought he was singing or messing around, like he always did, to get our attention." The image haunts me: he wasn't singing; he was dying. And so my sons and I each mourned alone.

A decade ago I sat down to write about the gifted musician I'd been married to. I chronicled the facts and dates and famous names relating to his life in music. But I did not capture his spirit. I went on to another attempt but this proved to be a Pandora's Box of my life, and I abandoned that too.

Last year, I set about writing a simple portrait of the man whose life had been entwined with mine since childhood. I summoned him up day after day. Rather than romantic reminiscence, I wanted to give as clear and true an account of the man he was as I could; using the language that accompanied my memories, trite or clichéd as it may now seem, because it was the language of the times we lived in. It took me a long time to sort through all the remarkable things I had witnessed and knew about him. I wrote only what was essential, with the guiding principle that less is more. Mark Twain memorably wrote to a friend: "If I'd had more time, I'd have written a shorter letter." I published the portrait and received grateful responses from many who had known him, as well as those for whom he had been an inspiration.

It had taken years of denial and escape to admit how much I missed my music-loving, freedom-loving husband. I had been defending myself against all the feelings I had buried and the demands he had made to live life to the fullest. He passed on to me the legacy of always being one's self; of taking hold of the life we are given. Albert Camus, who suffered from tuberculosis all his life and also died young, at age forty-seven, in a car accident, said: "In a world that doesn't make sense, live to the point of tears."

"You have a book in you," he had said, not long after we parted as husband and wife and moved into our 'great friends' stage. I had always wondered what book he thought I would write. Perhaps it is the one I am writing now: a broadening of that portrait into a story about the two of us.

 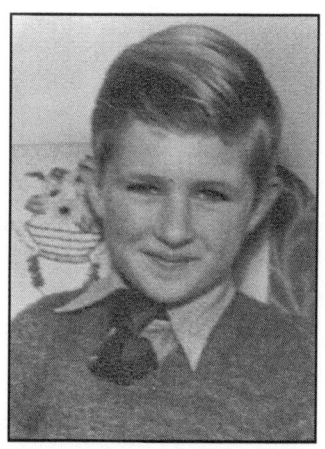

1

Our story began in the seaside town of Brighton, in the rolling green county of Sussex, in the thick of World War II. He was born in November 1941, in the county hospital. I was born six months later, in May 1942, in a nursing home.

I learned the things I shall write now about those early years, long afterwards, and not always in detail. After two world wars, people did not care to think or talk much about the past, or the lives of either their close or distant relatives. I remember being curious about my own family members and receiving only scant replies to my questions. Though the Englishman's keen sense of privacy played a part in this reticence, the past contained too many memories of death and loss and deprivation to want to discuss them. When peace came, people looked to a promising future, not to the past.

At eighteen, Gary's father, whose given name was Edgar but who was always called Eddie, enlisted in the RAF and went off to serve as a fighter pilot, unaware that his young wife was pregnant. The grandparents-to-be stepped in and purchased a semi-detached bungalow on a hill near the Hollingbury Park Golf Course, with a panoramic view of Brighton and the English Channel. There, they would keep company with their daughter and grandson until the end of the war. The two-bedroom bungalow with its neat front and back gardens had been built in the 1930s as part of the middle-class expansion that had been happening since the end of World War I—'the war that was to end all wars,' they had said.

The grandparents were publicans, running a busy ale house in a neighborhood of Victorian villas called Queen's Park, on one of Brighton's seven hills. Gary's mother, Audrey, a pretty petite blond with vivid blue eyes, would have helped out and learned to be outgoing and friendly with customers, not a typical trait for English girls back then.

By the time I met the grandparents, many years in the future, they were in their eighties. The grandfather was tall and pale, and always wore a hand-knitted Fair Isle V-necked sweater over a long-sleeved shirt. He wasn't one for many words, but was quick with a wisecrack and a mischievous smile. The grandmother made up for her husband's reticence with gossip and complaints and a similar impish smile. They seemed to be at a loss to understand what had happened to bring them to this place—idle after much activity, enveloped in their fireside armchairs, consigned to their sitting-room.

During the war, the grandfather, given the nickname Ginkie by his grandson, explained how his father was away being a pilot, and bought him model airplanes to demonstrate. The young boy took this as a sign, and would run through the bungalow, from back door to open front door, arms outstretched, attempting to take off. If his father wasn't there, he would at least emulate what he was doing.

In photographs taken at the time, Eddie was a handsome young man, with a shock of short black hair, dark eyes and startling black eyebrows. He had been born in Bristol, on the border with Wales, to a father who sang in a Welsh male choir and who, as a civil engineer with Wills' Tobacco—the maker of Woodbine cigarettes—was sent with his family to Portugal, to open a new factory.

After spending the first ten years of his life abroad, the young Eddie returned to England speaking not a word of English and with the look of a foreigner about him. The family settled in Brighton, a town boasting fresh sea air and many attractions, and opened a tobacco and sweet shop close to the seafront promenade. With music in his blood, Eddie's father soon tired of being a shopkeeper, and together with a friend, opened a musical instrument sales and repair shop. The shop—Windo-Martin Music—was in a prime location in Duke Street, in the old Regency part of Brighton, and was the only one of its kind. The shop did so well that Eddie left school at fifteen to work there with his father as an apprentice. His own love of music was encouraged with weekly lessons on accordion at London's College of Music. His choice of instrument echoed back to his childhood in Portugal where every band had an accordion-player.

When the war ended in 1945, Eddie was de-mobbed from the RAF. Despite having flown in many far-flung and dangerous places, he was sound in mind and body.

Back in England, the war had drastically changed the course of everyone's life. Austerity was still in force, with ration books for food, joblessness, and general lack of money. Eddie was luckier than others. He returned to work with his father in the music shop, ready to earn a living for his new family. Fortunately, the Englishman's habit of playing music at home was still alive and well.

◆

A photograph of my own father and mother, taken in Brighton the year before war broke out, shows them on their wedding day, my mother looking serene and my father on crutches from a motorbike accident.

My father's name was Aubrey, shortened to Aub, to sound

less posh. He was a slender man, good looking, weather-tanned and always well dressed. His father had been a Liberal politician who had died, prematurely, from tuberculosis, when my father was just two. He'd been born 'unexpectedly,' twenty years after two siblings who so spoiled and cosseted him that he always retained the charm and innocence of a child. In the halcyon years between the wars, he played guitar and banjo at Sherry's dance hall, and was a member of *The Pirates v. The Gentlemen*, dressing up and staging pirate fights in rowboats off the Brighton beaches, for extra income.

My mother was slim and quite a beauty, with brown eyes and dark-brown bobbed hair. Her father had been a Royal Navy yacht designer, her mother a coloratura soprano. They had named her Muriel Tempest after the opera singer Marie Tempest, a name my mother had soon discarded in favor of Betty. She had been taught to play piano so young, she couldn't remember when. At eleven, her life had taken on the drama of a Jane Austen novel: with both her parents now dead, she was delivered into the care of a strict Victorian spinster aunt who was a devout Methodist and a keen archeologist.

When war came, my father was not drafted because of a groggy heart; namely, a heart murmur. The terrible blitz of London went on, from the fall of 1940 until the spring of 1941, and my parents stayed put in Brighton. By the time I was born, in 1942, fears were growing that Hitler was planning to invade from the south coast—he had even taken photographs of Brighton Pier—prompting my father to take my mother and me to stay with his sister in Essex. Here, eleven months after my birth, my sister was born.

There was a short period of quiet on the home front until the first 'doodlebugs' began raining down. To protect his family from these terrifying flying bombs, my father decided to take us further away, to the safety of a farmhouse in North Wales. "They also serve who only stand and wait," was a line from poet

John Milton, used by Winston Churchill in one of his inspired war speeches.

At war's end, we returned to the green suburbs of Brighton. With the small inheritance left to her by her spinster aunt, my mother bought a modest house. My father, now suffering from a nervous breakdown, found that keeping tropical fish calmed his nerves, and on a gamble, opened a tropical fish shop, which he named The Preston Aquarium. It was the first in our town, and he quickly made a go of it.

With a business to run, my father gave up playing guitar professionally. Sometimes, I remember—because I so enjoyed it—he would pull out his guitar in a fit of nostalgia and get my mother to accompany him: "Ramona... When day is done, you'll hear my call...we'll meet beside the waterfall...." Or, to make my sister and I laugh, he'd strum away, singing: "...How in the heck can a fellow wash his neck, if it ain't gonna rain no more?"

My father must have taken me to Eddie's shop to purchase strings and picks because I have a fleeting memory of the window display, of dark wood shelves and cabinets and a glass counter on which the instruments brought in for repair were examined. The two men would have been nothing more than polite over the purchases, neither imagining that one day, each would become father-in-law to the other's child.

Eddie on the other hand was musically ambitious, and in addition to working in the music shop, branched out to form a twenty-man accordion band. Accordion bands had become popular, an offshoot of the cinema organs that everyone loved. Eddie clearly didn't give a hoot about the critics' disdain: "A gentleman is someone who knows how to play the accordion but doesn't!"

Many years later, I came across a sepia photograph of the band showing rows of accordion-players wearing tuxedos. Gary's mother is playing piano and looking glamorous. Her son, now six years old, is sitting behind a full drum kit, smiling confidently, too young apparently to doubt his ability to keep time for a professional big band. His father had already made sure his son wouldn't be hampered by stage fright or the words 'I can't.'

At age four, he and I began our education in the same infants' class at Balfour Primary School. One of my first memories is of my mother waiting for me and my sister at the school gates. Gary's mother is standing with her, chatting; her hand on the pram that held his baby brother. Even as a child, I sensed that both women were content as stay-at-home mothers. Neither of them worked outside the home, other than helping out at their husbands' shops on busy days. His mother had endured the fear of losing her husband to the war. My mother, orphaned at an early age, wanted nothing more than a home and family.

As children, he and I were luckier than we knew. In those early post-war years, we absorbed the sense of relief and freedom that was in the air. Out of school, echoing that freedom, our parents gave us free rein, left us to games of our own imaginations, out in the streets and fields until sundown. We were so free that I perceived it a great irony—one of the unsolved mysteries of the grown ups' world—that we were discouraged from 'showing off,' a taboo akin to a sin that I later understood to be at the root of the Englishman's reserve. This constraint about showing-off affected us all. Thanks to a father who'd known a livelier lifestyle on the Continent and did not fear swimming against the current, it did not affect Gary.

We remained in the same class all the way up school, though we knew little about each other outside the classroom and playground. Girls and boys eyed each other as different species: boys played rough games and their clothes were always mucky, while girls played dainty games and strove to look pretty. "What are little boys made of? Snips and snails, and puppy dogs' tails...What are little girls made of? Sugar and spice and all things nice..." goes the nursery rhyme.

But I remember him distinctly, one of only two boys whose existence I deigned to acknowledge. There was at that time a strong sense of uniformity, so that I was fascinated by those who seemed different. In response to my endless questions, my mother once remarked that I'd been born asking why? I noticed him because of his eyes: pale hazel, bright and intense, they expressed something that, to me, even as a child, felt like kindness. He seemed older than the rest of us, as if he had already seen more than we had. I had no words for it then, only a sense that he was ready to take life full-on, in a way other children were not. I couldn't know—and I didn't think to ask him later in life—if being so different made other children shun or mock him.

The eight-year-old boy must have felt some attraction to me, too, since he accepted an invitation to my eighth birthday party. I was pretty, with straight fair hair wound into plaits, and blue-green eyes. I wore a pink satin frock with a pink angora bolero, both of which my mother had made. It was May, sunny, and we were in the garden which was set out with beds of perennials, a narrow lawn in the middle, several small goldfish ponds and a large aviary. At the bottom of the garden, there was a tall overgrown bramble hedge that I would scramble through to reach the green playing fields of Varndean School for Boys, the school his father had attended.

My mother was organizing hunt the thimble and blind man's bluff and I recall wanting the party to go exactly as planned, taking the task of hostess seriously. Gary, however, seemed oblivious of this protocol. I have a mental snapshot of him veering off on his own to explore, and of my being vexed. He wasn't joining in the way one was supposed to, already less concerned with fitting in than with following his own impulses.

◆

While he was playing drums, I was mad about ballet, and all kinds of dance, especially wafting around Isadora Duncan-style in a chiffon tunic, improvising my own steps. My mother entered me into ballet competitions that made me nervous to shaking point, though I sometimes placed third or runner-up. But it was alone at home, when everyone had gone out, that I really danced. I'd seen Norma Shearer, my first role model, in *The Red Shoes*, and would set the LP of *Swan Lake* on our Dansette record player and spin around the living-room in a way I could only do when no-one was looking. These secret performances gave me the confidence to put on dance shows in front of the garage with my sister and our friends, our audience, the kind neighbors I had politely roped in. The shows were my way of sharing something I loved to do, and going against the unspoken ban on showing off.

By now it was 1953—and that June, we watched the Coronation of our lovely young Queen Elizabeth II on our first black and white TV set. We invited the neighbors, and all sat in rows, like in the cinema. I recall too my surprise when everyone in our street came out of their front rooms for what seemed like days of street parties, setting food on the longest communal tables I'd ever seen and talking to each other in such friendly terms, I thought I was dreaming. I had grown up hearing: "An Englishman's home is his castle," which until then had seemed to aptly describe my retiring countrymen.

Just five days before the Coronation, Edmund Hillary and Sherpa Tenzing captured the world's attention with their heroic climb to the summit of Mount Everest.

In school, we faced the terrifying specter of the '11+ exam' that decided the future of our education and our lives, in one fell swoop. Gary failed the exam and was sent to a secondary modern school that was also our town's first co-ed, a concept seen by most parents as 'new-fangled' and a risky proposition.

I managed to pass the exam and went on to Varndean School for Girls, across the fields from Varndean School for Boys. Passing, to my mind, was a questionable achievement since it resulted in my being taken out of the dance class I so loved. The reason I was given: "You'll only end up in the chorus, and what kind of life is that?" That this was said so that instead of becoming a chorus girl, I would make an acceptable wife for a doctor or solicitor went right over my head.

I continued to hear Gary's name mentioned because my sister failed the exam too and was sent to the same co-ed. I recall her telling me he had taken up ice hockey, and wasn't at all surprised: hockey was a fast and challenging game from across the Atlantic. By then, while most boys were stuck with short-back-and-sides haircuts and dull utilitarian clothes, he had his own version of a crew cut and wore the colorful shirts and jackets his father had bought during wartime leave in America.

From what I heard, he spent all his free time at the ice rink which was in the Sports Stadium on West Street, just around the corner from the music shop, above which his family now lived. He would watch the American and Canadian players who came over to compete against the Brighton Tigers, the National Champions, and was soon a good enough hockey player to be picked for the junior team. For extra pocket-money, he helped the lighting technicians during the ice shows.

I saw him once at the rink. I had gone one Saturday morning with my school friends. After the delicate ballet shoes, I hated the heavy boots and metal blades, and the cold air, and did not progress more than making a few awkward rounds of the rink. He, on the other hand, was clearly in his element, racing around in a padded jersey, his eyes full of enthusiasm and confidence.

The gap between us had widened so much there was no longer any point of connection. Our shared school days were over, and of course we thought nothing of it. Life had us in its grip, and on we went, on our separate ways. But there was something that neither of us could have understood then—the characteristics of the man and woman we would become and the things that would eventually draw us together were already there. The Jesuits' maxim says: "Give me the child for seven years, and

I'll give you the man."

There was too the great divide that girls were up against, whether they knew it or not. We were raised to behave well, to be virgins, to be wives and mothers. Boys, meanwhile, were raised for action and derring-do, and for working hard to make money. While I'd been persuaded to give up dancing, he already had several strings to his bow. These were the circumstances that marked our two destinies.

2

What I have written so far about myself is as true as any memory can be. Memory is a mechanism that selects and stores those things that stand out; as if we know they will add, at some point or other, to either our enjoyment or our understanding of our lives. I shall continue in this manner.

About him, I am at the point when I can only write what I was told later—by him, his family, and his friends. It will serve as a bridge to the next time our paths crossed and I shall write first-hand again.

In his years at home, from a young boy on, the house was filled with his father's favorite music, the brassy and boisterous sounds of the big swing and jazz bands—Duke Ellington and Count Basie, Artie Shaw, and Benny Goodman. The common taste of the time had become more conservative, calmer; everything was about not rocking the boat because the boat had been rocked so hard for so long by war. People were gathering their lives together, recuperating, finding jobs and opening businesses. Black musicians playing wild jazz had little to do now with an Englishman's life, and were rejected in favor of easy-listening vocalists like Perry Como and Dean Martin, backed by smooth orchestras; and Broadway show tunes from Cole Porter and Irving Berlin.

But then, in the mid-1950s, as we turned into teenagers, America sent us its rock 'n' roll revolution and caused a mutiny that had been a long time coming. It was a mutiny whose rhythms and lyrics urged us all on—girls and boys alike—to sexual awareness and the encounters that, until then, shame and shyness had made too murky to negotiate.

The world as I had known it had been essentially sexless; ruled by sexless adults, or adults who kept sex such a secret it was invisible. It was impossible as a thirteen-year-old girl to relate to Hollywood's sex symbols, film stars like Marilyn Monroe and Jane Russell. Their thrusting curves and titillating gestures were symbols of sex but far too removed on the screen to inform me about sex itself. The young princes of rock 'n' roll made sex, or at least sexual energy, palpable.

Gary, too, had taken one look at Chuck Berry and Bill Haley—at their raw guitar sounds and raunchy movements—and shelved his drum kit in favor of electric guitar. In the family garage, he rehearsed with friends, turning up the volume, letting rip in loud release from suburban reserve and ennui.

His father teased his son about the banality of rock 'n' roll and doggedly continued to lead his accordion band. Most parents were more outspoken, seeing this brash music as a sacrilegious scourge, a temptation to sin. My own hovered noncommittally rather than disdainfully, as they usually did, as if reticence on the subject would make it go away, at least give it less importance—which of course it didn't.

Rock 'n' roll brought liberation from the last vestiges of Victorian stuffiness. We bopped and sang and shouted, discarded our dull clothes and begged our parents to buy us the kind of sexy outfits the young singing stars were wearing. We became different people. The cultural cleavage between my parents and me was now a seismic fault that I knew would never be joined again.

Those teenage years were a sort of schizophrenia: the angst about whether to be like one's parents, or be like oneself. The problem being, one didn't know who one's self was, or could be. I enjoyed my school studies and was doing well. But rock 'n' roll had got into my blood. The young black singers with their easy sense of rhythm and loose-limbed dance routines and catchy choruses sang exactly what we felt. Frankie Lymon and the Teenagers' plaintiff, "Why Do Fools Fall in Love," hit the charts just as I was sobbing over the first boy who'd kissed me, and who'd promptly vanished. Little Richard and Jerry Lee Lewis were great for dancing to at friends' homes when their parents were out. And when I watched Johnny Ray writhe around the microphone singing and crying, "Just Walkin' in the Rain," he made me want to cry with him, never imagining he was putting on an act.

I fell in lust with Elvis, with his deep, sweet, and sensual voice and the never-before-seen way the man moved his hips. It was hard to believe anyone could sound and be that sexy: I could sense, if not name, the danger. We had our own English Tommy Steele and Cliff Richards, but they seemed harmless in comparison to Elvis.

Scotsman Lonnie Donegan, on the other hand, had a powerful effect on me, with his 'dishy' man-next-door looks. When I finagled my way backstage at the Brighton Hippodrome to get his autograph, he called me "dear" and set my heart aflutter. Meeting him in the flesh confirmed that the men making this great new music were actually real! I was so smitten with Lonnie and with Skiffle, my father made me a tea-chest with a gut string, and I got my sister playing a wash-board and a friend a comb and paper kazoo. With this atonal combo, we played along to Lonnie's hit, "Rock Island Line," and it was then that my father made a thoughtless but irreversible joke about my not being able to hold a tune. The idea that, all this time, at school, and in front of my friends, my voice had stood out for being tuneless, mortified me. From then on, I mimed whenever there was any singing, hymns at school or carols at Christmas. "Out of the mouths of parents..."

3

When he knocked at my door, sixteen years had passed since we'd last seen each other. He stood in the damp night, like someone who'd been beamed down from another planet. He was wearing a U.S. Navy Pea coat, and looked at me with a mixture of self-assurance and vulnerability.

It was October 1969, three months after the first moon landing, and two months since the Hippies had stormed Woodstock. He was now twenty-eight, I was twenty-seven.

He was half smiling as he waited for me to register the shock. He didn't know my mother had called to tell me he was coming. In an instant, I compared the man I was looking at with the boy I'd known. He'd changed a lot, but given a moment or two, I would have recognized him anyway, from his eyes, still as bright and intense as they had been. He was well-built, compact, but not tall; his fair hair had turned brown and was longer, and he'd grown a mustache and sideburns.

According to my mother, he'd popped into my father's shop that morning, had told them he'd just come back from the States, and had asked after my sister. On hearing she was married, he'd asked after me. I knew that back in school, he'd had a crush on my sister. My mother's call had been more of a warning, no doubt one of concern as I had just filed for a divorce from my husband. But as well, she'd always felt a very English aversion to Americans and everything American, accusing them of being loud and brash, and laughing at the Bermuda shorts they so often wore.

"Oh, my goodness," I said. Politeness more than anything made me invite him in. He took off his coat and sat down by the blazing coal fire. "Nice place," he said, in an American accent. There was an uncomfortable gap between what we knew about each other and what was unknown. "I heard you got divorced, and you got two boys, right?" he went on, and then we began to swap questions. When he saw we had a lot to say to each other, he went out to fetch a bottle of wine.

I was usually more restrained but felt a warm sense of relief as we shared our stories. We had come from the same place, at the same time, and we'd both been on long journeys, though neither of us had known where the other had gone or what we'd done. We were back where we'd begun, in our hometown, sitting side by side. "Yep, it's on the sea, right on the sea. I was born close to the sea. And my wife was born...right by the sea. We were born very close together, that's why we like to work together... We were childhood friends," he would say many years in the future, in an interview.

◆

I was only too aware of being a mother, alone. My sons were three and four. I was in limbo, about to be a divorcée, with no idea what my next step would be. I vaguely hoped I'd meet another man, but I wasn't in a rush. That evening I didn't for a moment imagine it might be the man sitting next to me; looking back, it was as if I had been waiting for him to arrive.

We went back in time together, to catch up from where we'd left off. I shall not try to fabricate the exact things he and I said, but shall simply summarize the gist. I seem to recall him telling his story first.

He was seventeen when he left home, "to see the world." For him, it wasn't to escape the stifling homes that other teenagers were suffering from, but to broaden his horizons. He had visions of being a pilot like his father, and tried to enlist in the RAF. Poor eyesight let him down. Instead, at the suggestion of a friend, he joined the Merchant Navy.

He'd met Ian in Brighton's Whisky-a-go-go café. They were both wearing American-style clothes and haircuts. Ian was astonished by how much his new friend already knew about America, the music, the cars, airplanes and railways. Both dreamed of going to America, and knew the Merchant Navy would be the only way to get there; without money or a job, it would be impossible.

By the time he left England and set sail, he'd already moved on from rock 'n' roll and had exchanged his guitar for a tenor saxophone. The big band jazz sounds he'd grown up with were coming to claim him.

For the next few years, he worked as assistant cook on various ships, including the Royal Mail Lines, and on various ocean routes. On the long passage to Australia on the SS Oriana, so as not to drive the crew crazy with his first screeched attempts on saxophone, he practiced for hours in the ship's meat-cooler.

Among the photos I was given years later by his mother, there was one taken on board that showed him as an eager-looking youth: the sailor on his Odyssey. In another, he is on deck, bare chest and tanned, his crew-cut hair bleached by the sun. And in another, he is sitting on a bunk with his sailor buddies, a set of bongo drums between his legs. Ian is showing the camera the pin-up girl on the cover of a magazine. The Merchant Navy was a society of men without women.

I met Ian eventually; he said, compared to his gifted and charismatic friend, he saw himself as his "side-kick." He told me how it was Gary's evening job to cut and prepare bacon for hundreds of breakfast meals, and how after that they would share one saxophone, to practice scales and tunes. He said Gary was so keen to improve his sound he devised a scheme to get rid of this old saxophone and buy a new one. In Sydney, he insured the old one, and then threw it overboard, thinking it would sink. To his surprise, it floated and was picked up by a passing boat, and delivered back to him.

The motion of the ship as it moved through the ocean waves must have stimulated his sense of freedom and imagination. His saxophone—or his 'axe,' as jazzmen call it—was always at hand; his lode star, his love of music. He did not tell me, so I can only imagine, what the boy becoming man felt as the ship followed its course.

On a cruise-ship port-of-call in San Francisco he finally went shopping for a new saxophone. He'd gotten to the point of practicing the tricky riffs played by jazz saxophonists John Coltrane and Charlie Parker, and many others. He had enough role models to last him a lifetime. But it was Trane and Bird who were the messengers of the new American Bebop style, and he was hell bent on understanding and playing it. He had a knack with all musical instruments but the tenor saxophone had staked its place in his heart and would remain his lifelong love.

In 1962, when he turned twenty-one, after plying back and forth between New York and Bermuda, his ship, the SS Ocean Monarch, docked in New York Harbor. He seized the moment and quit the Navy. He was at long last in the right place, the city he'd always dreamed of, his mind set on being a professional jazz musician. In the early Sixties, the Big Apple was a daunting and dangerous place to begin a new life, without contacts and with little money.

Soon after, Ian jumped ship; that it was the Queen Mary he was jumping, did not deter him. The two friends moved into an apartment in Queens, a gritty mostly black neighborhood, and set about realizing their shipboard plan: their own jazz combo which they named, The Mellow Browns, because it was a mix of

English, Chinese and African-American musicians. The group's first booking was to play in a sleazy club from midnight until eight in the morning.

He knew what hard work was, cooking for hundreds of passengers every day on board ship had taught him that. His playing progressed, thanks to Mike Petrillo, a saxophone player and teacher with good credentials.

He was ready to sweat it out in the New York jazz scene: sitting in with any jazz combo that would let him, to get the feel of it all, and be seen and heard. He went on the road with R&B bands, earning next to nothing but learning much. He found experimental workshops, and got another teacher, Warne Marsh, a white tenor sax player known for his 'cool' style. When he wasn't on the road, he practiced with a vengeance, and spent nights hanging out in jazz clubs. Soon he was playing in a group led by bassist Tommy Potter, who, with Miles Davis and Max Roach, had been a member of Charlie Parker's Quintet. He met and played dates with Maurice Waller, Fats Waller's son, and got to know Mary Weiss, of the Shangri-Las, before they made it big with, "The Leader of the Pack."

During the years he was getting 'his chops' together in New York, things were changing drastically back home in Brighton. People were working hard to move up in the world, acquiring goods, buying homes and cars. Even his father bought into the new economy: he sold his music shop and took a more lucrative and steady job with an instrument factory on the new Hollingbury industrial estate, a concrete sprawl on the outskirts of town that everyone saw as 'progress.' His mother got a job too, to help purchase the bungalow next to the grandparents, leaving the town center to form a family enclave in the quieter suburbs. "But that's the price we have to pay for stability," wrote Aldous Huxley in 1932, in his prescient *Brave New World*. "You've got to choose between happiness and what people used to call high art."

✦

While his love affairs had been with music, mine had been with men. Despite the first liberating effects of rock 'n' roll on girls, it was still men—and, therefore, boys—who held the keys to what I was looking for. As for my choice of a boyfriend, I didn't see myself with any of the Teddy Boys, Mods or Rockers, which narrowed my choice considerably. By then, French studies, and a school exchange to France, had given me a taste of a new identity. And so I pretended to be French, as if being French would solve my uncertainty. Naturally, it was to French boys—who came over the Channel to Brighton in droves to study English every summer— that I looked for *un petit ami*. "The grass is always greener on the other side of the fence..."

When I set my sights upon a particularly handsome and tanned French boy, to my amazement, he liked me as much as I liked him. It was 1958, I was sixteen, and we had our own summer of love. He took me in his arms and lay me on the green grass; it was a virginal initiation that was just what I'd been waiting for. In the throes of passion, he asked when I was going 'to do it.' I told him when I was seventeen. "I'll be back next year then," he said.

1959, the year I turned seventeen, was a highly-charged year for world news. We watched America launch its first Earth-orbiting satellite, and looked on as Charles de Gaulle became President of the New Fifth Republic in France. Khrushchev became Premier of the Soviet Union; Pope John XXIII was crowned pontiff, and Elvis Presley was conscripted into the U.S. Army.

These world events were duly noted, but my thoughts were elsewhere. My French *ami* kept his word and came back, but I had to tell him I'd met someone else. My new love was a man ten years older than me, a tall and lanky Bohemian poet and existentialist with shaggy hair and a long Roman nose, who I would later see resembled Bob Dylan. I had been drawn to him instantly, one day, in the street. I stayed because he saw who I wanted to be, not who I thought I was. One by one, he opened the doors into the worlds of music, art, theater, and film. He began with Mahalia Jackson's Gospel songs, and Big Bill Broonzy and Lead Belly's gravelly folk music. And when he first made love to me, it was to The MJQ's smooth and moody, *No Sun in Venice*; transforming that much-feared moment into something magical. "If music be the food of love, play on," wrote Shakespeare in one of his Sonnets.

Our love affair had nothing to do with marriage. As well as discovering the joys of sex, he gave me a rounded education. We saw all the French and German New Wave films, all directed by men—Godard, Truffaut, Chabrol, Fassbinder, and Herzog. Theater in London came next: the first production of Samuel Beckett's *Endgame*; Laurence Olivier's performance in Eugene Ionesco's Rhinoceros, and at the other end of the spectrum, the opening of *West Side Story*. There was too a jazz recital by Dudley Moore at the 100 Club after which, tired and perspiring, Dudley recognized my Bohemian and came over, to say hello and shake our hands.

I felt as if I were on a ghost train in the dark; with strange and wonderful things coming at me on every side.

He brought me books too, to go with my French and German studies: the Romantic poets, de Nerval and Ronsard; writers Camus, Gide, Sartre, Nietzsche, Goethe, and for good measure, Henry Miller. He left delicate embroidered handkerchiefs among the pages, and tiny cards with quotations. One read: "To be pretty and passive is pathetic." Another, a quote from Paul Eluard, read: "Real poetry is included in all that does not conform to that morality which, in order to maintain its order and prestige, builds only banks, barracks, prison, churches, and brothels." Both cards were much-needed clues to what I felt going on around me.

But my Bohemian posed a sudden fork in the road: which did I believe in?—my parents' rules of good behavior and polite society, or the wilder shores of poetry? Though he had fostered my new identity and my yearning for art, he did not know how to engender in me the belief I could become an artist myself.

By now, school felt like a prison. Still the Francophile, I had discovered Francoise Sagan's book *Bonjour Tristesse*, and the songs of Juliette Greco, the Bohemian chanteuse who at the time was in a passionate love affair with Miles Davis. I envied and admired these French women and caught a glimpse of myself in them. I sat up at night in my 'baby-doll' pajamas, reading and listening to their music, until I finally resolved to leave school, and then go to Paris.

But before I left, my mother insisted I attend secretarial school to have a skill 'under my belt.' I did it but hated it, and even got a job in a typing pool for three months. I was reading Sartre and found inspiration in his explanation of existentialism: "...the waiter in the café plays with his condition in order to realize it." I found the idea of being 'oneself' a revelation.

It was at about the same time that Gary had embarked on his merchant marine adventures that I took a ferry across the English Channel and arrived in the City of Light. With only the fifty pounds in cash that my father had seen fit to give me, I found a cheap hotel and set about looking for a job. The au pair situation I was offered came with a room of my own and a small stipend. On days off, I browsed the Left Bank book stalls and wandered the Tuileries. I spent evenings at the cafés, Les Deux Magots or La Rhumerie, and went on afterwards to dark jazz cellars, or took myself to L'Olympia music hall to hear concerts with Thelonious Monk and Miles Davis; the mastery of their instruments and the sweat on their black faces etched deep in my memory.

✦

When it came time for me to leave Paris and go home, I found my Bohemian with another girl. Living in provincial Brighton was out of the question, so I went up to London, landed a job in a language school, and got myself a miniscule bed-sitting room in Belsize Park. By the summer of 1960, now eighteen, I'd fallen in love again, this time with an impossibly handsome dark-eyed Tunisian student. When he flew home, I saved and sewed some summer clothes, and went to join him in Tunis in his family's home by the Mediterranean.

It was the year The Beatles performed their first concert as The Beatles in Hamburg. In England, Princess Margaret had married Antony Armstrong-Jones after her ill-fated love affair with the divorced Captain Peter Townsend. In America, John F. Kennedy had beaten Nixon in the presidential race. In Tunis, I had put myself beyond world events, political and otherwise.

My month's vacation turned into a much longer sojourn. It was easy living in Tunisia in those days, President Bourguiba had emancipated women, there were no veils; I barely knew I was in a Muslim country. The sun and heat I had so longed for in chilly England, an affectionate extended family, and the sensual rhythms and quarter-tone Arab music, went straight to my body. I stopped reading and for the next three years became a hedonist—eating exotic foods I hadn't dreamed existed, dancing with my belly and hips, and making love in the afternoon. In the absence of the pill, this activity led to two abortions and a sense of sorrow that would forever lie heavy on my soul.

That my Tunisian lover was as woman-loving as he was fun-loving eventually became intolerable. It was the spring of 1963, and I was about to turn twenty-one, when I fled North Africa and went home to Brighton. My father might have said I'd "gone off the rails," but he was too pleased to have me back, and refrained. After three years in a desert land, England was a shock to my system, the weather, culture, and of course, the music. The Fab Four had had their first hit, "Love me do," and Beatlemania was thick in the air. I remember being puzzled, even scoffing, at the popularity of what was then a rough and ready sound; perhaps because my taste had moved from rock 'n' roll to the sophistication of jazz and the complexity of Arab music.

My sister and my friends were either already married or about to get married. For the first time, I began to contemplate the idea of being a wife instead of a wanderer. And before I knew it, I met a man who seemed to fit the bill, and whom my parents approved of. I was getting ready to go out with him when my mother, who was listening to the radio, called out the terrible news that President Kennedy had been assassinated.

◆

While Gary was gripped by his jazzman's life in New York, soaking up all the newest sounds and working on the latest techniques, I gave in to the social order of my milieu and got married. My husband, who was several years older than me, was very English, good-looking, and liked to play classical guitar. Before I married him, shame made me tear up all the photos of 'my past.' We bought a bungalow on a quiet suburban street—not far from Gary's family's bungalow—and a green Mini Cooper.

I gave birth to one baby boy, and eighteen months later, to another. I washed nappies and cooked three meals a day, even started a chapter of the NSPCC; unaware or in denial how far off course I had drifted.

Just as Gary's mind was set on playing like the great jazz giants, I was determined to be a good mother and housewife.

I was still ensconced in motherhood when, in 1964, Queen Elizabeth gave birth to her fourth child, Prince Edward, and the pirate station Radio Caroline began broadcasting, taking over from the old Radio Luxembourg, the only station that had brought good pop music to us when we were teenagers. Tuning in to the radio brought rare moments of feeling in touch again, moments that marked the cultural era, and of forgetting I was marooned in suburbia.

I would sometimes dance about the bungalow to The Dave Clark Five's Bits and Pieces, and listen to Dusty, "...It's crazy but it's true, I only want to be with you," and to Petula Clark, "Downtown... You may find somebody kind to help and understand you." Though I considered myself happily married, the urge to get outside the box was still there, unsatisfied and unnamed. *"Nous vivons dans l'oubli de nos metamorphoses,"* wrote Paul Eluard. We live in the oblivion of our changes.

4

That evening, sitting by the fire with my childhood friend, in a pause in our tête-à-tête, it occurred to me that it had only been a few months before, in the summer, that I'd been sitting in the back garden of the marital bungalow and a sudden vision of all the years ahead had come to me, with the awful thought: "Is this all there is?" I had carried on with my life and forgotten the thought. But not long afterwards, a carpenter had come to make renovations to the bungalow. He was, like me, married with children, and we found ourselves immediately attracted to each other. Though it seemed at the time to have come out of the blue, for me, the infidelity signaled the end of my marriage. And now, here I was: there *was* more to life.

The fire was down to its last embers, and we had finished the wine. There was a chill in the room, and his mood changed. He had said nothing about a wife or girlfriends and I hadn't asked. Now he sighed and told me how he'd fallen in love with a girl from Barbados and had married her. He said she'd gotten pregnant immediately, and because they were penniless, had an abortion.

"She died of nephritis," he said, shaking his head. "After that, I got hooked on heroin. All the jazz guys were doing it. But

I couldn't stop." And then, glancing at me to gauge my response, he added quickly: "I'm not using now though."

Despite my lovers and travels, I knew nothing about drugs, and had no idea what being a heroin addict meant. I could see he wanted to tell me the whole story. He'd been arrested for selling a small amount of heroin to a narcotics agent, and had served the past year in New York's Rikers Island jail. He told me, with a grim smile, his prisoner number—769-3107, unit 5U—as if it had been tattooed onto his brain.

"It wasn't all bad though," he said, with a grin. "In jail, they gave me a saxophone and a chair in the prison band!" The chair, he explained, had just been vacated by Shafi Hadi, a musician who had played with the legendary bass-player Charlie Mingus. Some of the other prison band members had played in Charlie Parker's groups—all of them jailed for heroin possession.

In a strange twist, while I was writing this part, his friend Ian sent me some of the letters he'd received, written from jail, on sheets of prison paper. It was twenty years after Gary's death, and they were shocking to read; partly because I felt I was invading the friends' past privacy. But also because, in them, I saw the man I'd lived with at the most crucial moment of his life, and though it was a bittersweet discovery, knew him even better because of it. Had I read them when we first met, I might not have felt such compassion.

The letters began: "My dear brother," or, "Well, old bollocks." And then, looking out at the weather from behind prison bars: "It's finally cooled off. And we have some sweet gentle rain, beautiful, eh? I dig it very much." As I read, my eyes filled with tears. In all the years I had known him, he was never one to complain or blame others for what he'd done, and here was further testimony. He wrote of meals: "Chow has just been called. I wonder what apatizing [sic] morsels will be set before us this evening????[sic]." He reported back later, "...scrambled eggs, spuds and carrots...it was okay."

28

He caught up with news: "Yesterday, I watched the Apollo II take-off on TV...imagine if man were finally to become spacemen...how I wish I could travel in outer space, but I guess for now I have to continue my journeys through inner space, in the tunnels of my mind."

But the pages were mostly filled with musical pointers to encourage his friend. He worried that in his absence, he would lapse in his studies. He had copied out the complex Bebop modes and chromatic half-step blues that he'd picked up in the jail band. To me, they looked like hieroglyphics or algebra, a mathematical prowess that floored me.

He wrote too how privileged he felt to have learned so much from his fellow inmates, and saw it as a gift he was obliged to pass on. "Once I can talk to you...I believe I can finally begin to teach a little."

In later years, when we were together, I would often wonder why he encouraged me so tirelessly, and encouraged so many others. Now, I understood. "By learning you will teach; by teaching you will understand," goes a Latin proverb.

In the last letter he writes: "...time is speeding, now only twenty-five more days! I can't believe a year is almost gone." And before he closes: "This has been the greatest experience in my life, man. It's a shame that this is the only place where you can gain so much experience...a few months back, I never imagined I'd be blowing solos alongside Shafi...it's such a gas to play Bird's old tunes with cats who blew with him! Just a little time to go, and much knowledge in my head, I'm excited."

He always signed the letters: "I wish I could be with you, digging the free life. All my love to all the beautiful people. Love from Little Bird," with a tiny cartoon of a bird, in honor of Bird, the master: Charlie Parker.

When the year was up, he'd been deported to England, his life in America over.

I took in all that he confessed that first evening without alarm or judgment. When he left, around midnight, he asked when he could come again. I hesitated, to put him off, aware perhaps in my bones of the epiphany he would bring. He wasn't what most young women of those times aspired to, either as a romantic date—a handsome man, preferably with a red sports car—or as one that would lead to marriage—a good man, with a steady job. And yet, I had never talked to anyone in such an open and honest way. Maybe next week, I said, and walked him to the door.

I remember him telephoning the next evening. He tried to conceal his eagerness with a joke, about bringing some alligators for my boys. I laughed, thought him pushy, but found myself saying I was cooking dinner and he could come if he helped. Now that I was alone managing the children and the chores, as well as two part-time jobs, my perfect housewife's perspective had shifted.

I worked a lunchtime job as a waitress in a newly-opened American-style buffet restaurant, and in the evenings typed documents for a solicitor I'd worked for before having my babies. In marriage, I'd been taken care of financially. I was now poor, having no savings and having agreed to a small child-support payment because I had been the one to leave. I paid my father five pounds a week for the bottom flat of a house he'd bought to ensure a roof over his daughter's and grandsons' heads. The house was a solid Victorian red-brick semi-detached, with a sunroom and a back garden. As well as an eat-in kitchen, there were two large rooms: one, my living-room-cum-bedroom, the other, the boys' bedroom. Before my father installed a proper bathroom, I washed the boys in the kitchen sink and used the outdoor toilet.

He was at my door in a blink. We prepared the meal, with a lot more commotion than usual, and then we all sat at the kitchen counter to eat. He easily endeared himself to my sons because he was still a boy himself; the boy I'd known when I was their age. He asked them about their favorite things, he listened, and made up silly jokes to make them laugh; they laughed even more because he kept bursting into cartoon-like laughter himself. The boys had so far accepted without upset the move and their new living arrangement, perhaps because the separation had happened without a long contentious lead-up, and there'd been no arguments in front of them. They were seeing their father each weekend, and showed no signs of anxiety about the arrival of this new man, whom they simply called Gary.

As I get to this point, I cannot say if I felt his presence in those first days as a threat or a blessing. He was clearly a threat to the conservative status quo I'd sunk into and was in the process of rejecting once again. He was a blessing precisely because of that.

I do not want to gloss over the hard parts of our life together, nor make them seem worse than they were. It is not so much how to find the truth, but where to find the courage to write it. Ernest Hemingway told Martha Gellhorn, when she complained that she didn't know how to write: "There is nothing to writing. All you do is sit down at a typewriter and bleed."

✦

Divorce was still frowned upon, and brought a sense of guilt and shame to the woman concerned. Gary had unquestioningly immersed himself in music, had long ago chosen his path and stuck with it. But I was now grasping at anything to help me understand what had happened to me.

I had been listening to Bob Dylan on and off since the mid-Sixties: it would have been hard for anyone to miss, "Blowin' in the Wind," and, "The Times they are a'Changin." Now, he became my poet-preacher, and *Blonde on Blonde* my inspiration: "...and your magazine-husband who one day just had to go...who among them do you think could destroy you? Sad-eyed lady of the lowlands."

Dylan's looks and lyrics reminded me of the French poets I had so avidly read. His message—that there was another way to live—was the opposite of the songs that had filled my teenage years: "Love and marriage...they go together like a horse and carriage," were the bouncy lyrics Alma Cogan had sung back in 1956.

I let him move in with us. He simply arrived a week or two after first knocking on my door, carrying a small canvas bag, its sole contents the few belongings he'd left jail with. Along with the bag, he was holding a black case that contained the Selmer tenor saxophone his father had bought for him when he'd seen how well his son now played, and how dedicated he was.

From the first evening, he found his place and set a tone that fitted in well. He was the Pied Piper, playing his saxophone all round the house. While I did the chores, he'd play the BBC's "Music While You Work" theme; and for the boys, it would be "Bill and Ben, the Flowerpot Men."

When I was at the waitress job, he went looking up old pals and musicians and would take my younger son with him. The child had loved music almost since birth, and had even been born to music: at the crucial moment of a home-delivery, I'd hummed and tapped, "The Grand Old Duke of York," because of its strong percussive rhythm. After the excursions with Gary, my son would return home speaking jazz jargon to his brother—"Hey man!" and, "I dig!"

Gary dazzled us with his cooking too, rustling up American soul food; a favorite was pork chops with collard greens and black-eyed peas. He made what seemed to us huge amounts, a habit from his days as ship's cook, but brought the boys to the table with keen and curious appetites.

It wasn't long before I began to feel redundant, and then resentful. Cooking had been a big part of my housewife's routine, and I had taken a certain pride in it. It took a while for me to realize he had handed me a gift: a break in my relentless routine, and a chance to take stock of my life. Years later, in 1992, when

Leonard Cohen sang "There is a crack in everything, that's how the light gets in," I thought back to those first days with Gary, and how he'd made that crack in my life.

✦

I knew he didn't have a penny to his name, and he understood my financial situation was tight. Apart from that, we didn't discuss money, and it didn't occur to me to ask him to get a job because I understood his heart was set on earning a living with his music. How he would do this, I had no idea. In that respect, he was lucky; we were lucky: there was less emphasis on money in those days. The austerity of wartime had eased but it had left its mark. No one frittered pennies or pounds, 'making ends meet' was still the order of the day. I'd had to learn to fend for myself, away from home on my travels, and empathized with those who'd done the same. Any distrust I might have felt was suspended by his kindness, his single-mindedness, and his refusal to make excuses for his circumstances.

At the end of the day, when the boys were asleep and I was typing, he took to being DJ and putting the few jazz albums he possessed on the turntable. With the music, he reminded me of that other person I'd started to be, in another lifetime.

I recall that one of the first albums he played was Miles Davis' *In a Silent Way*, just recently released, and the first to cause a controversy about fusing electric rock with jazz. Gary was surprised and pleased that I'd heard Miles play live back in 1959, when I was in Paris; and that I even remembered him playing "'Round Midnight," and "Bemsha Swing." Once you'd heard those sultry haunting notes you never forgot them.

He and I were on the tenuous cusp of a new life. We'd both found our way back—from Africa and America—to our families, who'd accepted us without recrimination. We visited them in turn, on Sundays. We walked a fine line—eager to show them who we were—or thought we were—but respectful of their ways.

His parents and grandparents still lived in the adjacent bungalows up on the hill by the golf course. When he took me to meet them, I saw it was a shock. The young girl they'd known was now a grown woman, and the woman their son had found so soon after returning home. Seeing him after so many years had been shock enough.

His mother was still the attractive woman I remembered from my childhood, and her sparkling home was a testament to her taste and industriousness. In her kitchen I would help prepare meals; making tea and sandwiches provided an excuse for her to ask discreet questions about her son, and how I was getting on with him.

His father talked and laughed a lot, drank espresso coffee and liked to smoke a cigarette, and was unthreateningly opinionated. I did not remember him—it was mothers, not fathers, who had figured most in my childhood—but I took to him immediately. He liked to tease me and I saw from the glint in his eyes that he had a way with women. I recall thinking that flirting was perhaps an expression of his need for freedom, and that he hadn't completely given in to domesticity. He still played the big band albums with the hi-fi volume up, filling the bungalow not only with

1969, Gary and me, in Gary's parents' garden in Brighton.

the upbeat music but with his animated presence which made his home seem too small to contain him.

At my parents' house, things were less animated. My father liked 'peace and quiet' after dealing with the noise in his shop. My sons had an affectionate bond with him because he told them stories and taught them his favorite pastime, fishing. He would try valiantly to strike up a conversation with Gary, focusing on music, at a loss what else to talk about.

I helped my mother in her kitchen. She would chat about the shop and the neighbors, and ask me about the boys, but bit her tongue about my living with a man out of wedlock, as if it would not bear calm discussion.

My sister, Joy, and his brother, Graham, veered between amusement and annoyance at our unconventional ways. We may have seemed over-confident to them, especially in the expression of our various ideas, given that they still held firm to the conservative ways.

✦

Each day in those first months, my life changed before my eyes. I'd buried the audacious girl who'd set off on travels abroad and now his lust for life was bringing that audacity back into my life.

He noticed details, talked to people everywhere, how and where he felt like it, even when it was not the 'thing to do.' He spoke to the dustman and the bus conductor in the same way as he spoke to the vicar who lived next door, and greeted our family doctor with a cheery, "Hey Doc!" when he made a house call to check on the sudden bout of asthma Gary experienced.

The local shopkeepers, who were the authority on our daily bread, meat, fish and vegetables and commanded a healthy respect, took a while to warm to his ebullient approach, to his quips and "Have a good day" Americanisms. "Man, those tomatoes are something else!" he'd say. With him, I saw that, despite my travels, I'd never really lost my English reserve: I was still an observer, not an actor in life's drama.

"Manners maketh man" is a universal maxim. But the English manners I'd been brought up with went too far. The rule was to keep oneself to oneself, as if others weren't interested in anything one had to say. Talk and gossip were carried on behind curtains, not in the street. Being polite was like being dumb. "Politeness is organized indifference..." wrote Paul Valéry.

During this period I found that sex, too, took on a different aspect. His life had taken him beyond romantic notions. I sensed that for him sex was sex, and love was love, that the two sometimes but not always, went together. I'd broken the taboo of sex before marriage. But I was only half way there, having been mostly passive to men's desires and fantasies. He saw me as a person first, and then as a woman he desired. He would hold me tightly; he was strong and passionate.

Something of the sensuality of my life in Tunisia came back, when music and making love had been inseparable. One evening, I took out an album of Bedouin music and danced for him in a flimsy slip, tying a sash around my hips and thrusting them to the darbouka drums' pulsing rhythms. I was revealing another lost part of myself that the man in him appreciated.

My father and mother had never shown the slightest hint of lust or desire in front of me. Like the other adults I knew, they had gone along with the facade of distaste with which society viewed sex; at least, public sex. Any hint of it on TV would be viewed with embarrassed silence or titters.

It had been easier for Gary, his father had seen to that: sex was evident in his father's expressive physique and his instinctive interest and self-confidence around women. About his son's previous sexual experiences, I still knew nothing. I didn't ask, and did not see until much later that I had re-ignited his libido after the devastation of heroin and the celibacy of jail.

It was about this that we had our first argument.

One evening, he brought home a couple he'd made friends with in a pub. The man was a photographer of nudes, the girlfriend one of his models. She was dressed provocatively off-camera, too; a see-through blouse, a tight black mini-skirt, and black thigh boots. Her long fair hair hung over her pale face. I was caught off guard, still wearing the more sensible clothes of a housewife. Looking at me as she stroked his arm, as if to detect any jealousy on my part, the girl said, "Isn't he a cool guy?" I responded with a tight smile and watched him soak up her charms. I had left my Tunisian lover because he'd had eyes for all women; the last thing I wanted was to go through that again.

When the couple left, I shouted and slapped his face. He told me to stop, grabbed me, and pushed me against the wall, bruising my arm. When I had calmed down, he put his arms around me. "Come on. You're my old lady," he said. I'd heard that jazz musicians spoke of their woman as their "ol' lady," so I accepted it as an endearment and a rite of passage.

I came to the clear conclusion after this quarrel that there were two ways to be with a man. From what I had already experienced, there was passionate, alive, and jealous; or calm, routine, and longing for passion. He had made me angry, made me see that I was out of touch with the new open sexuality. It was time to 'get with it.' I started by buying a pair of tight brown velvet jeans, a buckled belt, and sassy boots. Along with these, I abandoned my chignon and let my long hair loose.

Bearing all this in mind, and aware I couldn't cope with more babies, I asked my doctor to put me on the pill. Though it had been available to married women since the early 1960s, I'd never considered using it. I didn't like the thought of interfering with my body's rhythms, and would only stay on it for a year.

5

It was a Sunday lunch time, the first time he sat in with a band. The pub was in a back street, down near the seafront, and was packed with people, and filled with the smells of beer and cigarette smoke. He introduced himself to the band leader as an "expat American," in an unmistakable American accent. It was his way of holding on to the identity he'd forged while paying his dues in America. After the band had played a string of jazz standards, he got the nod that he could sit in. He put the reed into the mouthpiece and looked at me, "You okay?" he asked, as if he wanted to make sure I'd be all right until he got back.

I, too, felt unexpectedly protective. How would he play? What would the crowd think? Half way through the number, he took his cue and delivered a solo that began smoothly and built to a wail of atonal notes and runs, the most powerful, and painful, sounds I'd ever heard. I'd heard him blow free-form at home, but not with the same volume and intensity. The last high-pitched crescendo almost threw me back in my chair and brought the pub's noisy customers to silence and stares. He finished the solo to loud applause and whistles; and to more than a few frowns.

Sitting there alone, I was proud of him. But he seemed like a stranger; I'd never been close to anyone who displayed such talent. It was one thing to go to jazz concerts, quite another, to listen to the man I lived with. He came back to the table, sweating, grinning, and a bit breathless. He asked what I'd thought, and I said it was great. And I knew he would soon go from jams in backstreet pubs to greater things. And that I would be there when he did.

Gary, wearing the hat I knitted for him.

As I wrote this, I saw that it described everything about him, at that moment. He was making up for lost time, using all the pent-up energy from being a heroin addict and being in jail—all the wonder and pain of his life were coming through his horn. He knew he'd been given a new lease on life. He knew, too, what it would take me some time to see: every time he went on stage to perform, he was leaving me.

At home, he practiced constantly, endless scales, and playing along to records. I soon recognized the fast Bebop licks of John Coltrane and Charlie Parker, and the fiery bursts of notes from Pharoah Sanders. The young Eric Dolphy was a great influence on him, too. And Ornette Coleman, with his vocalized alto sax screams. But I sensed that it was the mournful melody of Albert Ayler's "Ghosts" that resonated most deeply. He would play the tune over and over, as if to make it his own. "These cats began the free-form jazz movement," he said. But he loved all music and had an especially soft spot for funk: Horace Silver's fluid piano playing on his album *Song for my Father*, and Lee Morgan's soulful trumpet on his mainstream hit single "Sidewinder," from the album of the same name.

As much as jazz had gotten into his blood, rock 'n' roll was still there too; with the sounds that had 'shaken him up.' He took us both back to our teenage days with growling licks from Fats Domino's "Ain't that a shame?" and Little Richard's "Long Tall Sally." A decade or so later, in the midst of his most experimental free-form jazz days, he would say: "I'd grown up playing rock 'n' roll... I wanted to play an extension of that. I didn't want my art to be inaccessible."

Sometimes he would slip into the blues, catching me unaware with notes of heart-wrenching smoothness, or belt out strident runs from King Curtis, or Sly and the Family Stone. "Boy, those cats are cooking!" he'd say, taking a breath before plunging back into blowing. I danced around the flat listening to Sly's hit: "Everyday People...a butcher, a banker, a drummer and then. Makes no difference what group I'm in. I am everyday people." Dancing and my natural sense of rhythm had never left me. It had been my first means of self-expression, and remained a constant in my life.

But it was Alice Coltrane's piano-playing that prompted a monumental change in me, with all the movement and freedom she expressed. "Freedom is an internal destination of the heart," wrote Zora Neale Hurston.

One evening, while I was typing and listening to *Cosmic Music*, without stopping to think, I said, "I'd love to play piano!" I must have thought, how terrible to be sitting typing, while Alice's fingers created a river of such entrancing music.

"Then we'll get you one!" he said. I reminded him that I knew nothing about music. "That's not a problem," he said. "I'll teach you."

When the upright piano I bought from a newspaper advertisement arrived, he kept his word, instructing me in rudimentary scales and simple chords that I practiced in between my jobs, household chores, and looking after the boys. Even at night, in bed, until my eyes closed, he would test me: "How many flats in G-flat? And how many sharps in E-major?"

The idea of learning to play at my age was daunting. The piano seemed like a mountain waiting to be climbed: how would I ever translate the pleasure of listening and dancing to music into playing music? I bought a beginner's book with exercises but soon got depressed with my mistakes. "Okay. Don't get crazy. Forget scales for now," he said. "Let go and play anything you feel. Think of dancing. Let your fingers dance on the keys. Get to know the sounds a piano can make." He had chosen the right words—my hands were part of my body and my body knew how to dance.

As I had done as a child with dancing, I would wait until he had gone out to practice and let go, driven only by the sounds my fingers made on the keys, in a sort of improvised physical language. About this, he would one day say in an interview: "I've sort of had to take the saxophone to pieces and blow it inside out. The same applied to the piano for Pam...the way to get the sounds you want...you have to get beyond the instrument."

He was my lover, my friend, and now my music master.

He inspired me; and, like him, I was eager to make up for the years I'd lost.

He had come to me at the right time, just as the most creative free-form and fusion music was emerging and flooding the music scene in England and America. Had this not been the case, I would not be writing this book. Freedom to express oneself and create was the new chant. It was in the air. You no longer needed permission or approval to express what you felt; you could create something new in any art form you chose.

While I was struggling with my first musical steps, he was way ahead, had already taken great strides in modern jazz. Now, he was hungering after more experienced musicians, and a broader choice of venues than our town could offer.

◆

Inevitably, things got difficult with my parents. I'd chosen to leave the safety of my marriage and had allowed a penniless jazz musician to move in with me. I was once again going off what my father called, "the straight and narrow." But now, instead of being out of sight in some far-off country, everything I did was in front of them. At least I knew that, for his parents, I was the answer to their prayers, a roof over their son's head and someone to care about him.

My father came each morning, to drive my elder son to school on his way to his shop. One morning, I forgot to close the living-room door, so that when my father glanced into the room he caught sight of the long bump in the blankets on the couch that doubled as our bed.

"He's just an out-of-work musician," he warned me, the next time I saw him. I had no defense prepared. "Well, it's up to you. But don't come to me for money," my father went on, with the nervous authority of a self-made man.

He was a self-taught musician as well, a fan of Django

Reinhardt and Stephane Grappelli. He'd heard Gary play when I'd asked him to bring his saxophone on one of our visits. He'd played a few bars of straightforward blues, which my father clearly approved of; but he'd finished with a blast of atonal notes that caused my father to comment to me later, "And what kind of music does he call that?" When I said it was free-form improvisation, he was blunt. "But there's no melody," he said.

But the new man his daughter had chosen was so full of life and so good with his grandchildren that he restrained himself from further criticism and simply hoped for the best—as he had always done.

But there were soon other things that drew criticism. I went flying with the solicitor in his Cessna: "And what do you think would happen to the boys if it had crashed?" I took in the friend of a friend who'd been thrown out of her home because she'd been diagnosed with schizophrenia. When she took an overdose in my flat and was admitted to hospital: "Why would you take such a foolish risk?" they asked.

It all came to a head one day with two clichéd and painful phrases: "After all we've done for you!" uttered by my mother and father in unison; followed by my response: "Fuck all you've done for me!" As the words came out of my mouth, I knew I had drawn a line that could never be erased. Twenty-seven years of emotional and dutiful attachment ended in that moment. I wondered what they would have thought if they'd listened to Dylan's appeal: "Come mothers and fathers, throughout the land, and don't criticize, what you can't understand, your sons and your daughters are beyond your command."

When I confessed to Gary what had happened, he said: "Hey, babe. Maybe it's time you broke away from your Mum and Dad!"

He had already wagered the price of freedom, and knew only too well it did not always include the comforts of home or the approval of family. I had seen how he stood his ground, always remaining stalwartly himself, without resorting to disrespect or impertinence. I had chosen my path alongside him and would learn to stand my ground too.

It would of course have been easier to defy my parents had they abused me, or not cared about me. I might then have become a total tear-away. But it was a good family, and the stamp of family is a permanent dye. Part of me wanted to make something similar, but something with more freedom and creativity at its center.

This radical change in my behavior may have had something to do with my first taste of marijuana, and the buzz of awareness that came with it.

Gary was by now going to London for a day here and there, and had started to meet influential musicians. One weekend, he invited an American drummer to stay. Barry Altschul was at the time the drummer in Circle, along with jazz icons Chick Corea, Dave Holland and Anthony Braxton.

He was a wiry young man of about twenty-seven with bushy dark hair and a full beard. I found him interesting and earnest. He'd just come from Paris and a series of performances. I would have liked to say something about my own days in Paris but the two men were so caught up in their jazz talk, I couldn't get a word in edgewise.

"It's okay. You don't have to if you don't want to," Gary said as he handed me the joint Barry had rolled. Whatever vestiges of reserve or prudence remained suddenly crumbled: with one drag of the joint, I felt my mind and body floating away somewhere. I'd finally got stoned at the age of twenty-seven. I went to the mirror to see if I looked as different as I felt. I recall staring at my face and hands in the glow of the candles I'd lit, incredulous to see every detail, every line, vein and pore. And here, not surprisingly, the memory ends.

Our paths never crossed again, though a month or so later, in London, Gary would introduce me to Chick Corea who was sitting at his piano, looking weary at the end of a gig.

His trips to London became more frequent. He didn't have the cash to buy a train ticket, and didn't ask me to buy it for him. Instead, he rode the bus down to the main London road and with his black saxophone case in hand—that a wary driver might have taken for something more sinister—put out his thumb. He usually made it back home late at night, the same day; full of stories about where he'd been and who he'd met.

There was one night that stands out, when I was in bed, waiting anxiously for his return. Around midnight, I heard the loud grind of gears and the revving of an engine in the silent street. He had charmed a truck driver into bringing him right to our door.

He was bold in approaching musicians, using his engaging sense of humor as well as a feel for being in the right place at the right time. It was a mystery to me how he knew where to go. On one of his first expeditions, he had found his way to the Roundhouse where he'd sat in with Jack Bruce, during Graham Bond's all-star *Sun Festival*. Until its break up the year before, Jack had been the bassist of the mega-rock band Cream.

He would head too to Ronnie Scott's, the newly-opened club that had become the hub of British jazz. He met plenty of musicians who congregated there to chew the fat, share tips about where to sit in, and which groups were looking for personnel. One of these was the legendary saxophone player, Johnny Griffin, who took Gary on to play a couple of gigs with his quintet.

I remember deciding I wanted to go to London with him. We splurged on tickets and went by train. At the Café des Artistes on the Fulham Road, we met up with Steve Florence, a young guitarist Gary had met. Steve was a rock fanatic as well as a jazz enthusiast. Gary felt an immediate connection and the two of them were already talking about forming a group.

The Café was at the time 'the place to be.' I was looking around in the dark for David Bowie and the Rolling Stones because Steve said they sometimes dropped in. It was exciting to feel the energy of the city and of people out to take it all in. Later that night, we drove to Steve's flat and sat with him and his wife on their living-room floor, talking and listening for hours to Jimi Hendrix's *Electric Ladyland*; Pink Floyd's A *Saucerful of Secrets*, and the Beatles' *Yellow Submarine*. After that night, my snooty reservations about rock music in general, and the group from Liverpool in particular, became a thing of the past.

6

By the summer of 1970, he had asked and I had agreed to move to London. At first, it had seemed a drastic thing to do, for the boys, who were now four and five, and for our families. But with his increasingly frequent overnight trips, it seemed to make sense, and I was beginning to feel left out. I'd enjoyed living in London when I was eighteen: why not go back?

On his next trip, he called me from a phone box to say he'd found a flat. I asked where, he said in North London, as if he'd stuck a pin in a map. "It's a great pad! But you gotta come up. The estate agent says I don't earn enough," he shouted excitedly, inserting coins as fast as he could. When he said the rent was three hundred pounds a month, I shouted back, that we couldn't possibly afford it; to which he said, not to worry. He said he'd met a musician named Robert Wyatt who was going to live with us and split the rent.

I had no idea how it would all be arranged. But Gary's enthusiasm proved stronger than my prudence. I called a friend to babysit, and the next morning I caught the train to London. I had no bank statements, only the reference and composure I'd acquired working as secretary for the solicitor. These, with my pink cashmere twin set and pearls, seemed to satisfy the estate agent that I was well in control of our (imaginary) finances.

We set off a few weeks later in a friend's van, the four of us squeezed into the front; our cat Eloise tucked carefully into a cat-carrier in the back. After crossing the whole of London, we arrived in the late afternoon at the gates of Brookfield Mansions, a distinctive three-story red-brick building at the bottom of Highgate West Hill. Between the two of us, and with the boys lugging toys and light items up the three flights of stairs, we got moved into our new home.

The flat was all white, from the walls to the floors. The casement windows were large and south-facing, and flooded the flat with light. There were three bedrooms, two balconies, a fifty-foot hallway, a large kitchen, a dining-room, and a sitting-room. There was even a store room that we would soundproof to make into a music room.

That he had recently quit a prison cell and yet had had the audacity to find us such chic digs was an indication of his devil-may-care approach. And for me, after the little bungalow and the cramped flat, it was the stuff of magazines. We were poor as church mice, but here we were in an upper-class flat overlooking Hampstead Heath, with views of the green hills rolling up to Parliament Hill. The common sense proverbs my mother had brought me up with always rang true. "Nothing ventured, nothing gained" was one of her favorites, handed down and used since Chaucer's time. "Where there's a will, there's a way," was another. I had joined forces with the irrepressible boy I'd known as a child. Between the two of us there was more than enough 'venturing' and 'will' for us to embark on this brand new life.

◆

I remember the day our flat-mate arrived. Robert Wyatt was the drummer with the art-rock group Soft Machine, a name they had borrowed from William Burroughs' novel. The group, that was continually changing its line-up of musicians, had its roots in the Hippie Movement and its founding members had been Robert, Kevin Ayers, Mike Ratledge and Daevid Allen, who were part of the artsy and literate *Canterbury Scene*. After a chaotic series of tours with Soft Machine in the U.S. in 1968, opening for Jimi Hendrix's ground-breaking Experience tour, Robert was moving away from the group to work on his own music.

He was polite, seemed on edge, and smoked a lot, and I was impressed that he didn't act like someone famous. To me, he looked the epitome of rock-world celebrity, with his straggly blond hair and crumpled pale linen suit that spoke of money. I had no idea it was his only suit, or that he was far from rich. I only recently learned that, in Robert's own words: "I was as broke as you were because Soft Machine management was a bunch of thieves."

That first day, I recall Robert looking around the flat, admiringly, and saying, "It feels like a grown-ups' place." I recall too that he handed me a bottle of Calvados he'd brought back from a recent tour in France.

Robert Wyatt, top center, with Soft Machine members, circa 1970: Elton Dean, Mike Ratledge, Hugh Hopper.

Gary was pleased to have his new musician friend close at hand. I went along with the arrangement not only because we'd share the rent, but because I liked the Hippies' notion of living with other people to share ideas and work. I'd been very taken by the kibbutzim as a teenager and had even contemplated going to Israel to volunteer. And in Tunisia, I'd enjoyed how open the homes were and how easily the extended families came and went.

Robert settled in, and brought his new girlfriend to visit. Caroline Coon was famous too; she'd started a foundation called Release that gave legal counsel to young drug offenders—a huge undertaking at that time. I was immediately in awe of Caroline; she seemed light-years ahead of me in a way I could not put my finger on. She was tall, with a full bra-less bosom (something still not generally done) that she clasped against her when she ran down the hall. Robert would dedicate the ballad "O, Caroline," to her, two years later, after they had parted; and in 1977, The Stranglers would compose "London Lady" in her honor.

Caroline and Robert babysat the boys one night when I wanted to go with Gary to Ronnie Scott's. The club was on Frith Street, opposite some shady sex joints, and seemed both mysterious and posh, with a dark brown frontage, an entrance of double glass doors and a side door for musicians. Ronnie Scott and his business partner Pete King, both tenor saxophonists, had hung out and jammed in New York clubs in the early Sixties and had created their club to provide British jazz musicians with a similar venue.

That night, as we walked in, I found myself standing next to Princess Margaret, wearing an ermine stole, out on the town with her friend Peter Sellers. The club was one of the places to go in London. Pete King gave the go-ahead nod to Gary, who of course was already known at the club: he was a hard man to ignore anywhere.

We were standing at the back, behind the tables, when without fanfare, Ronnie himself appeared on stage and the audience went quiet. He was an attractive man, graying, and diffident, and didn't appear to relish the limelight. He was famous for his dry humor, which was perhaps his shield.

"In just a few moments, what's 'is name will be back on

the stand," he quipped. "Meanwhile our waiters and waitresses will be pleased to take you-er-to take care of you," he continued, with the practiced timing of a musician. "You should have been here last week. Somebody should have been here last week! We had the bouncers chucking them in." And then, feigning embarrassment: "A guy rang up to ask what time the show started and I said: 'What time can you get here?'" As quietly as he'd begun, he introduced the musicians and left the stage.

Over the years, I heard so many famous musicians perform at the club—Charlie Mingus, Buddy Rich, Stan Getz, Airto Moreiro—that to remember the chronological year each played is impossible: they have all got rolled into one long show.

◆

Robert did not stay long with us in the flat. After a few months, he went to live with musician friends in a terraced house in Islington, in a more Hippie, less family-oriented setting. When he was there, he took up with Cyrille Ayers, the beautiful red-headed French ex-wife of Kevin Ayers. Robert had a way with women, and I recall him one day saying: "I like all women, there's hardly a one I don't fancy!" Given the attractive milieu he was a part of, that didn't surprise me. We used to go over a lot to see them; they lived in the kind of artistic chaos I could never give myself up to, so I'd help look after Rachel, the little daughter Cyrille had had with Kevin.

By then Robert and Gary had forged a strong bond and continued to thrash out their ideas for a group that Gary named Symbiosis: their vision, an out-and-out free-form jazz style mixed with rock—a wilder version of the new prog rock. Steve Florence was on guitar, along with Roy Babbington on bass, and Nick Evans on trombone. Gary composed a band signature tune, "Stand Fast," which had echoes of BBC programs. "That was my band and we were fucking great!" he would later reflect in an interview.

"Although he'd had a tough life even before I met him, Gary's music had the (almost!) innocent joy of a child, still full of wonder and excitement. He was nothing like most English jazz musicians: a rather guarded, suspicious lot in those days. He seemed oblivious to careerist ambition. And he had SOUL. He naturally absorbed both R&B honking tenor sax swagger, with the sensitive tonal nuances and courage of Archie Shepp...a complete musician." Robert sent these words to me, on hearing that I was writing this book.

It was Nick Evans who moved into Robert's old room. Nick was a Welshman with a whimsical sense of humor that chimed with Gary's Celtic background. Nick was one of the best trombone players on the British jazz scene. I was pleased, because he brought an element of calm with him, and would play for hours with the boys. He was also one of the few musicians who saw, and instinctively acknowledged my dilemma—of juggling being a wife, mother and musician.

During the years we lived in the flat, we never earned enough to not have to rent the room. But we got to enjoy the company of an array of artistic, temperamental, and international tenants—from a rock band's road manager, two demure Japanese students, a feisty Czechoslovakian girl, a bossy American woman, a young English abstract artist, a boxer—John Conteh, who became light-heavyweight champion of the world—and a pair of Aussie Hippies.

◆

In September of 1970, in that first overwhelmingly full year of living in London, we mourned the loss of two music legends of the Hippie era. Jimi Hendrix was the first to go, from an overdose of barbiturates. Coincidentally, his last live gig had been at Ronnie Scott's, sitting in with Eric Burdon's band, War.

Gary mourned the untimely death of one so young and so talented, and played "Star Spangled Banner"—a free improvisation if ever there was one—over and over, in a private requiem. Who had ever sung anything like, "Excuse me, while I kiss the sky?"

"I won't live long either," Gary said, in a somber tone. It was the first of several times he would say those words. I remember turning away with a quick, dismissive, "Don't be silly!"

Two weeks later came the news of Janis Joplin's death, from a mixture of heroin and alcohol, some suggested suicide. She epitomized for me the powerful women of the times who against all odds dared to express what they felt, and were raw and vulnerable because of it. "Don't compromise yourself. You're all you've got!" was one of Janis' refrains that struck home.

Her voice had the same powerful and painful strains that came through Gary's saxophone. There was no denying that drugs were taking their toll. It was tragic and reckless, he said. But there would always be victims among great artists, like great heroes in war, sacrificed to open minds and hearts all over the world. Aldous Huxley wrote in *The Doors of Perception*: "... The martyrs go hand and hand into the arena; they are crucified alone."

Our parents took drugs too, only theirs—alcohol and sleeping pills—had been legalized. Even my father kept barbiturates by his bed.

◆

On November 15, 1970, a week after his thirtieth birthday, Gary was booked for his first major engagement, with Centipede; an orchestra led by Keith Tippett, and called Centipede because of its fifty musicians. At the rehearsal I went to, the only musician I knew was Robert, who was one of the orchestra's three drummers. Among the others, Gary pointed out Keith and his wife, Julie Tippetts. As Julie Driscoll, she had been an iconic figure in the Sixties, skinny, and with an ultra-modern gamine hair-style and dramatic eye make-up. In 1968, she'd had a #5 hit with, "This

Wheel's on Fire," with Brian Auger and the Trinity; a remake of which became the theme for the TV series, *Absolutely Fabulous*.

He pointed out Robert Fripp, who wasn't hard to miss with his long wavy chestnut hair that rested on his shoulders and reminded me of King Charles I, an appropriate style for his group, King Crimson. The group's first album, *In the Court of the Crimson King*, was an ambitious mix of jazz, funk and chamber music, and the most influential ultra-progressive rock album of its time.

A few days later, I was sitting alone in the balcony of The Lyceum Theatre in London's Haymarket, nursing mixed feelings. Gary's life was moving fast, and as he stood on stage, doing what he loved most, and surrounded by people he knew, I felt a terrible pang of estrangement, and emptiness.

He was the opening soloist. I shivered as the sound of his saxophone filled the vast auditorium, instantly recognizable—a rainbow of tones from smooth and rich to staccato and piercing. The solo was electrifying, as if his body and horn were fused. What had sounded so alarming in the backstreet pub had found its rightful place. I could sense him stirred by all the space and by the audience's hunger to be moved.

"At the end of a gig...everybody's gone...all the energy that's been coming at you...is gone. Then you realize how important the audience is," Gary would comment some years later.

Backstage, afterwards, I couldn't get past the throng of musicians and their admiring friends and fans. This, I realized with a sinking feeling, would take some getting used to. I felt utterly out of place, as if I were invisible. He, meanwhile, was mopping himself off and seemed as relaxed as if he were at home.

He sat at breakfast the next day reading *The Times' review*. "...his solo was 'demented'...that of 'a madman.'" He chuckled, pleased as Punch, knowing it was better to be singled out as a madman than not to be mentioned at all.

Centipede members for the album cover.

Within a few days, he left for France, for two Centipede concerts at the Alhambra Theatre in Bordeaux, and another in Rotterdam. It was his first tour since he'd returned to England, and the first time he was away from home for more than a day or two. The flat felt so empty without him that feelings of abandonment came over me. My only solace was in my piano, the movement of my fingers over the keys, to create sounds to calm my anxiety. "There is a balm in Gilead...to heal the sin sick soul...if you cannot sing like angels...." was from an African-American spiritual. I would listen to a version by a well-known jazz singer, whose name I cannot now recall, that was truly a balm for me.

His return home was both a relief and a celebration, with stories and gifts. Roy Babbington, one of Centipede's bass players, reported: "We were going to France on a tiny chartered flight with everybody clinging to their seats except Gary, who was rushing up and down the aisle playing like Archie Shepp. He was trying to cheer us up about being in a rickety old plane...but I don't think it had occurred to us that we were in a rickety plane until Gary started playing!"

Quite often, he would arrive home without warning with fellow musicians in his wake, so that our flat was like a musical salon where ideas about new albums and groups found a place to be aired. The London music scene was an incestuous melting pot: everyone played with everyone else, and everyone had a group, a duet or trio, a quartet, or big band.

I remember one of those who came over was Mike Patto. Gary knew Mike from Centipede, where he was one of the five vocalists. He was a big guy, fun-loving, with a deep voice, and at that time was lead singer of Dick and The Firemen. He went on to form the group Boxer with Ollie Halsall. It was a shock and a loss to the music scene when Mike died a few years later, aged thirty-six.

Guitarist Ollie Halsall came over several times. At the time, he had his own band, The Blue Trafs (farts, backwards). Gary would sometimes sit in with them, and when Ollie got an album deal with the projected Ronnie Scott's label, he hauled Gary in to record with him. Robert Fripp, who produced the album, wrote about it some twenty years afterwards: "Ollie's album was recorded and very quickly – about three days. The problem was that when the musicians got together to rehearse, they got stoned instead." Needless to say, because of this, and lack of funds, the album was not released.

I remember quite well the time Ollie brought his wife to visit us; she was a slim pretty young woman who seemed much in love with her untamable husband. Ollie's zaniness hid, or rather was a symptom of, his genius. While playing at Butlin's Holiday Camp, where many an out-of-work musician paid his dues, and where it took a serious sense of humor and a passionate pastime to survive the boredom, he'd developed the 'four-finger hammer-on runs' that influenced many guitarists. I recall thinking that Ollie and Gary would have made a success as a comedy duo, the way the jokes kept coming, from slapstick to obscene. I didn't know at the time that Ollie was a heroin addict and shared his habit with his friend Kevin Ayers, whose band he would later join. Ollie would succumb to the drug, with an overdose at the age of forty-three.

From many of these musician friends, I learned that humor was the key to keeping on playing music in a society where everything was designed to keep things the way they were—calm and in line—and where the artist's limitless talents were rarely remunerated and mostly frowned upon.

At first, because the musicians were all men, I felt awkward, like an intruder, listening to their conversations in musicians' vernacular. He never mentioned what I saw, perhaps to not give it credence: that as well as starting to play music late in life, I was up against the status quo—the jazz world, like the rock world, was a men's club supreme. He also chose not to see, that in encouraging me, he was going against the club's rules. It was about then that Linda McCartney began appearing on albums and then on stage with husband Paul, who had taught her to play keyboards. The media and musicians alike sneered and made jokes. Paul resisted—as did John much later with Yoko—and kept her in his band. Despite the jokes, I saw myself in her, and vacillated between envy and sympathy.

A harsher fact did not escape me either: he would be more likely to succeed in his profession if he hadn't set out to take me and my sons on the journey with him. My sentiment was reinforced when, one day, quite without malice or forethought, a long-haired grungy-blue-jean-wearing roadie with a famous rock band responded to a comment I made with, "Men are already up against it competing with other men, let alone with women!"

I did not dwell on this because Gary's commitment to me was as dogged and passionate as his love of music. And as for taking on my boys, he was reliving the childhood he had so thoroughly enjoyed.

Between his practicing and mine, we managed to keep to a daily routine. I did most of the cooking for our family dinners—the favorites were curries, bluefish with broccoli, and shepherd's pie. But he'd cook too if he was home; bustling around, and getting the boys to the table. With him, everything was animated. Topics over dinner ranged from questions about the boys' schooling to guessing games, often conducted in hilariously exaggerated, Peter Sellers-style Indian accents that came from his movie *The Party*—"Birdie num-num. You mashuga! I am not your sugar!"

I suppose, in retrospect, we were like an ordinary family, though an ordinary family might not have agreed. He had a way of pretending to be mad at the boys, about their squabbling or not tidying their room. They'd listen, with bated breath, sensing he wasn't quite as angry as he made out, but never quite sure. On the odd occasion, if they were being especially pigheaded, he'd grab the two of them by the scruff of their necks, march them to their room and close the door.

I remember one day, he burst into a guffawing outburst in the entrance to our building, to aggravate some pernickety residents. The boys were with their playmates, and I overheard my elder son explain, "Don't worry. My dad's bark is worse than his bite."

He could be tough but was ingenious with it. One Saturday afternoon, when they had spent all their pocket-money on sweets and had eaten them all, he gave them an extra shilling or two and urged them to go buy some more. "Eat them all! It's okay," he said. The boys fell for the trick, until they felt so nauseated, they had to stop. He helped me enforce television-watching times—the number and kind of programs—and allowed no laissez-faire attitude about weekday bedtime.

◆

Christmas that first year in London—his second with us—was the first time we decided to stay at home instead of going to Brighton to celebrate with our families.

A week or so before, he had set to building the boys a rocket ship from two enormous cardboard cylinders he'd found in a warehouse in Kentish Town. As it had to be a secret he used the music room, which made it pretty cramped and too noisy for any serious piano practice. He painted the cylinders glossy white, put in a seat, a hatch, and a control panel with a rod to navigate among the moon and stars of the battery-lit universe that a fellow musician, Ray Russell, came over to help Gary wire up and install.

Ray was a gifted guitar player with whom Gary would have a long association. Ray had paid his dues with Graham Bond, Cat Stevens and Georgie Fame, and now had his own band, The Running Man, a mind-bending mix of heavy rock, R&B and free-form jazz. I recall Gary often playing as guest with the band for gigs in London and all over England

On that Christmas morning, the rocket stood next to the Christmas tree and appeared so large that when the boys first saw it, in half-darkness, with the trees' lights sparkling on its surface, they gasped and took a step back, thinking it might be real and blast off.

The toys he made for the boys, and the games he conjured up for them, excited him as much as it did them. He spent hours with them assembling tiny model airplanes, fastidious to the last detail. He bought them airplane spotter cards and tested them on each plane's data when we were on long car drives.

But it was revamping that was his forte. He got a kick out of fabricating a devilish-looking go-cart out of planks of wood, and painting it black, with orange flames. The boys would hurtle down Parliament Hill on it, and have to leap off at the bottom because he'd omitted to include brakes. In time, as they got older, he fixed up second-hand skate-boards and bicycles with Day-Glo colors and transfers, and would go out with them, making the excuse it was for test runs. The more daring their games became, the more concerned I was for their safety; divided as I was between hunkering down in the music room and wondering what they were up to. "They're boys!" he said. "They're born explorers. Don't watch them, or you'll drive yourself crazy!"

His insistence on my not worrying added to the process he'd begun and encouraged, of turning toward my own life, and to my piano playing. Though I never stopped worrying that they'd get hurt, he gave me permission to not be a perfect mother, whatever that was. I'd left that paradigm when I'd left my marriage. It was about then I asked the boys to call me by my given name; hearing them call him by his name and me, Mum, made me feel dull and old by comparison. They accepted this request as just another of those things parents did. Hippie parents had been doing that for a while anyway. "I want my life. I want it now. I don't want to give it to the next generation," Margaret Drabble had written, back in 1963.

◆

We had moved from living close to our families to exploring a musical community of like-minded souls. My parents came only once to visit us. My father detested driving through London, his worst fear, getting stuck in a traffic jam. When he and my mother saw with their own eyes that we were not living in a dump, they did not repeat the journey. "Yes, it's a nice place," they said, clearly out of their comfort zone in our 'artsy' surroundings.

It wasn't traffic that prevented Gary's parents from visiting us more than once. They both worked full-time jobs and their weekend routine did not include traveling more than a few miles, to have lunch with friends, or go to a local pub for a Sunday jazz jam.

We accepted it was up to us, having moved away, to drive the sixty miles to visit them. We had by then bought an old VW Camper bus, the Hippies' emblem of freedom—of being able to take to the road at the drop of a hat, of independence, away from society's conventions and domestic rules. "Little boxes... And the boys go into business, and marry and raise a family, in boxes made of ticky-tacky, and they all look just the same," were Pete Seeger's much sung lines from 1963.

Having inherited the aptitude for mechanical things from

his father, he set to fixing the Camper up. I would lean out of the kitchen window to watch him in the tradesmen's drive below. Happy in his mechanic's overalls and covered in oil, with the transistor radio on while he worked, he would mutter and swear, "Where did I put those bloody screws and nuts!"

One Sunday afternoon, we painted the body of the Camper emerald green and the roof, yellow. We gave brushes and paint pots to the boys and let them loose to create a canvas of giant flowers, a sun and moon, and a firmament of stars on the Camper's sides. We refurbished the interior, and re-covered the seats that became a bed for the boys.

He would put on his pilot's sunglasses, and wearing our raggle-taggle Hippie garb, we'd set off on the main London to Brighton road, displaying the bumper sticker, "Keep Music Live." We'd arrive in a blaze of color, and park our incongruous bus in the drowsy suburban streets of our childhood.

7

Early in 1971, there was an upsurge in his career. He was in great demand, sitting in, or being invited as guest, with many progressive jazz groups. He performed with Centipede and with Mike Patto's band at the Lanchester Arts Festival. I recall too being in a London club watching him play with Jimmy Ruffin and his band. Ruffin, who'd had a big Motown hit with "What Becomes of the Broken-hearted?" was wearing towering platform boots and as he strutted across the stage crooning into the microphone, one of the heels fell off and left him in disarray.

And then, with Robert Wyatt's reputation, Symbiosis, the group they had formed together, got a series of breaks—a week's engagement at Ronnie Scott's, performances at the Country Club, and a BBC live recording. He had set his sights high, reached for the sky, and was thoroughly enjoying the ride. I'd had a dream when I first met him; one that I hadn't told him about and never would. He was long-haired and bearded—like Jesus Christ Superstar—and was zooming up to the moon on a rocket that disappeared into the heavens.

He had quickly placed himself in the forefront of the British avant-garde jazz scene. I wonder, as I continue to write, how he found the courage for all this. Audacity was his biggest asset and had been hard won—surviving the death of his wife, heroin addiction, jail time, and deportation from the country he loved. It had humbled him and forged his character: "...a desire to reduce a chaos of experience to some sort of order, and a hungry curiosity," wrote Graham Greene.

He had by then proposed to me several times. "Hey, baby! Let's get married!" he'd say, when he felt particularly enamored of me. I was leery because I'd not long got free of the first marriage, a mistake I quietly regretted. Living together suited my new perspective.

I finally accepted, and on March 1st, 1971, we drove to the Old Marylebone Town Hall in the VW Camper. The boys were with us, taking it all in their stride. We had two witnesses: our flat-mate Nick Evans, and Mongezi Feza, who played pocket-trumpet with The Brotherhood of Breath. Gary felt a special affinity with Mongs, as everyone called him. He had lived in a South African township before fleeing apartheid with The Brotherhood's bandleader Chris McGregor, and always seemed mystified, as if he hadn't yet got his bearings.

The marriage ceremony was simple, a relief, compared to the elaborate affair of my 'white wedding.' I remember Gary joking with the registrar, "What am I doing here?" I don't think he placed a wedding ring on my finger, as I have no recollection of ever wearing one. I did not put one on his finger either because men weren't wearing wedding rings in those days.

There was another surreal moment when the registrar said: "Congratulations Mrs. Feza," instead of Mrs. Windo, causing me a moment's shock and Mongezi's dark skin to turn quite pale.

A few days later, on March 6, on the First International Women's Day, four thousand women strode through the streets of London waving aprons, silk stockings and shopping bags. At the end of the march, they handed a petition for equal pay and equal education to Prime Minister Edward Heath.

Wedding day photograph at Brookfield Mansions. left to right, Mongezi Feza, me, Gary. Front row, left to right, my sons, Simon and Jamie.

Gary with our two witnesses, Nick Evans and Mongezi Feza.

The wedding photos were taken in the front gardens of Brookfield Mansions, with much posing. Gary was wearing a brown polo shirt, a waistcoat with turquoise satin appliqués, an African bead necklace, and a pair of striped pants in mauves, pinks and blues that I had sewn for him on the Singer sewing machine my mother had given me as a wedding present, and which I have kept to this day. When my father saw the photos—it was only afterwards we told our parents of the wedding, to avoid a fuss—he said the trousers looked like pajamas.

My outfit was a see-through silver-grey blouse, a green and maroon tapestry skirt, and a white hooded jacket edged with metallic gold embroidery that I'd bought in Tunisia. All things Eastern were part of a Hippie's wardrobe. I'd braided my hair overnight, to give it the unkempt frizzy look.

Mongezi sported a huge African purse with a long fringe and a floppy white hat that hid his face, except for when he smiled and showed his beautiful ivory teeth. It was Nick who looked the most respectable, in a short brown fur coat and brown tailored trousers. He was nursing a cut lip he'd got while playing with the boys before the wedding ceremony.

But the day that had begun so well did not end well. When we returned from the ceremony and opened our front door, a dozen of Gary's musician friends jumped out at us, shouting, "Congratulations!" Among them, those I recall were Marc Charig and his girlfriend Anne, and Julie and Keith Tippett.

He had planned a surprise, ignoring my own plan for a small family lunch. Since there wasn't enough food or drink in the house for everyone and since neither he, nor I, had much cash on us, there was a quick whip round to purchase more food and drink, a gesture I found embarrassing in the circumstances.

There was also the question of a surprise guest—the divorced American woman who had been the previous resident of the flat. I had met her when we'd first gone to view it. What was she doing here? I asked him, in the kitchen. She's lonely and sad about her divorce, he said. And with all that was going on, the music, the voices, the drinks being poured, I had to contain my doubts. Nick came to put his arm around me, to say he understood.

There was no avoiding that I had married someone who was at that moment in his life a very sexual being, as well as being a man who felt great empathy for the suffering of others. I could not judge him for this, but railed against the notion that with this combination, he would always respond to a damsel in distress. And I might never know how far the response would go.

✦

We had, day by day, without calling ourselves by its name, taken to the Hippie culture. Some of it I found too extreme—I'd never been one for extremism—so I only embraced what I deemed valid for our lives.

We rejected all aspects of the materialistic society we'd seen mushrooming since our post-war childhoods. We refused to follow our parents who had stepped so eagerly into the consumer age. We had no money to furnish our large flat and didn't care. I had brought the few pieces of furniture I owned from the marital bungalow. The only things we purchased were a spin-dryer and two double mattresses. These we placed side by side on the floor in the corner of our bedroom, with two colorfully-embroidered white candlewick bed spreads draped on the walls behind them. The bedroom was large with two windows that opened onto a balcony. Apart from mattresses, it was sparsely furnished: a dressing table with a three-sided mirror inherited from my great-aunt Mabel; a small wardrobe; a chair, and two plants that stood on the hi-fi speakers. It was a Hippie boudoir in which we would hang out and listen to music, as well as sleep.

As for clothes, while dull polyester and rayon had taken over the mainstream fashion scene, we adopted Hippie clothes because they were colorful, interesting, cheaper, and more comfortable! For everyday wear, we both went about in flared blue-jeans with knee patches that I sewed on. In summer, we wore frayed cut-off jeans.

Gary's dress sense was idiosyncratic but not ostentatious, his only fashion fixation a pair of red Converse All-star high tops, a rarity still in England, and not cheap. I made dressier trousers for him and for the boys using the Singer. For the boys' school clothes, we shopped at the low-cost C&A department store on Oxford Street.

My wardrobe included blouses of many colors, antique waistcoats, and Women's Land Army fatigues, items I would find at The Salvation Army store. A year or so before, in the haunting song, "Suzanne," Leonard Cohen had chanted: "...she is wearing rags and feathers from Salvation Army counters..."

My only splurge was on a pair of the knee-high gray suede boots made by Biba that were all the rage with the Mods and 'the beautiful people.'

It was fun, like dressing-up; as if we were reverting to a remembered state of childhood, to a time of pleasure and fanciful freedom. We naively honored the idea you might play—whether it be music, painting or writing—all your life, instead of being an office worker or bus driver.

As for money, it seems impossible now that we lived well on an almost non-existent income; we lived on air and ideas. On principle, we refused to apply for the dole. Nevertheless, we understood that to live like this, sacrifices and economy were necessary. "Take care of the pennies, and the pounds will take of themselves," was another of my mother's proverbs.

Kevin Ayers, who was at the forefront of the music revolution, said in defense of the Hippie movement: "The Sixties were the only time that young people got up and had any effect at all...until the establishment moved in and discredited them: 'They're Hippies, they don't wash, and they smoke pot.' But there were huge advances in human rights and basic freedoms. It never happened in the history of man, ever again."

A couple of times, when we were especially low on cash, Gary would go and busk in the echoing tunnels of the London Underground. I always wondered who among the crush of tired travelers would appreciate the finely-honed notes of a master.

If he collected a few pounds, as a treat he would bring home a bottle of Woodpecker cider, or a couple of lagers. Neither of us felt the urge to drink much, and didn't have the money for it anyway. We didn't smoke cigarettes; but we sometimes shared a joint with friends. As for anything stronger, he'd say, with great conviction, "I don't need dope. I've got you and the boys now." It was easy for me to believe him: that life was good without heroin and that being alive and playing his saxophone was more than enough. And it wasn't long before he began to earn modest sums from gigs and sessions on a regular basis.

My contribution to the rent came from a job as lunch-hour barmaid in the saloon bar of the Duke of St. Alban's pub across the street. I was careful with expenses, and didn't expect to go out to dinner. I took to baking bread and shopping for bulk brown rice and vegetables at a co-op, which led to us becoming vegetarians. We still ate fish, having grown up eating it fresh from the shore. I made vegetable burgers and 'meat' loaves, home-made yogurt and ginger beer. The boys had no complaints, but the vegetarian phase would peter out a year or so later, when I was rebuked for presenting a huge nut-stuffed green marrow instead of a turkey for Christmas dinner.

◆

On July 3rd of 1971, the music world lost Jim Morrison. The sexy exhibitionist poet-singer, the son of an admiral, bled to death in a bath in Paris, following a heroin overdose. As with Jimi and Janis (all J's, and all of them dead at twenty-seven), the cause was never clear. I had watched him, mesmerized, as he had sex with the microphone, in black leather pants, and sang: "Come on baby, light my fire..." How could any woman not have wondered what that fire would be like?

Sometime in the autumn of 1971, Gary brought home a houseguest. Alan Shorter was the older brother of Wayne Shorter; he wasn't as famous as his brother, but had recorded several albums with Archie Shepp, including *Four for Trane*. When I first met him, he had a homeless air about him that worried me. But I agreed to let him stay 'for a while.' Nick Evans had just vacated his room because he'd found a flat to share, and we hadn't got round to looking for another tenant.

Alan was an intense and brooding man, tall and wiry. We were instantly wary of each other; he was a Gemini, like me, and told me that Gary's sign, Scorpio, was the most powerful in the Zodiac.

"You're raw," was one of the first things he said. "You have no calluses for life." He was of course witness to my ongoing struggles with piano, and to my constant questioning of Gary about women, a habit that had grown worse with the endless nights he was now out at gigs.

Part of the reason for Alan's stay was that he had recruited Gary to make up a quartet to play in Paris for a live album. The other musicians were South African bassist Johnny Dyani and drummer René Augustus. A trip to Paris was too enticing to miss: somehow we had just enough money for me to go.

By late October, we set off to France. After a long ferry and train journey, when we arrived on the outskirts of Paris, the digs Alan had secured for us turned out to be in a disused wing of a mental hospital. Our Spartan room was off a long hallway that smelled of antiseptics and hashish. "It's not the Ritz, man! But it's cool," Gary said with typical cheerfulness.

The inmates were treated in another wing but when I looked out the window, a few of them seemed to have escaped and were wandering in the grounds, half-dressed, dropping their pants to defecate in the grass.

"They're artists and musicians who couldn't make it,"

Alan explained. "They're sick and tired and poverty-stricken, and came here as a last resort." It was quite possibly the hospital known as *Malmaison*—'sick house'—where Zelda Fitzgerald was admitted sometime in the 1930s, though I didn't know that at the time.

After a long rehearsal that filled the hallways with wild music—an apt symbol for all the unspoken emotions struggling within the patients—Alan's ensemble played a live performance for French radio at the prestigious *La Maison de la Radio*, near the Bois de Boulogne. In comparison to the wretchedness I'd witnessed beforehand, it was a glittering event: powerful music, bright stage lights, perfect sound, and a full house.

Afterwards, I met pianist Don Pullen, who I'd recently begun listening to. He was with the Art Ensemble of Chicago at the time, a group of black jazz musicians who were all living and playing in Paris. Proximity to those who have succeeded is a sort of aphrodisiac, and a good luck charm. The auditorium was bursting with the aftermath of male energy spent, of sexuality. I felt it, was drawn to it, and knew that sex and this music were inseparable. Although I cannot be certain, given the excitement of the event, I believe the performance had been recorded for the album Alan had planned, that would be entitled *Tes Esat*. Unlike the albums of his famous brother Wayne, Alan's would remain obscure, as was his death in 1987, aged fifty-five; but would be re-released in 2005. I was seeing the gamut of the music world: both the winners and the losers on the road to creativity.

It didn't escape me that often Gary would be the only white musician in a group. I recall him telling me he'd been asked if he'd ever felt any discrimination about not being a black jazz musician. His reply to this had been: "No, never felt it anyway. I'm white English from a Celtic tribe. My ancestors were wild maniacs who painted themselves blue, and fired arrows at the Romans, stuff like that."

◆

By the end of that year, Gary was playing regularly with the South African ensemble, The Brotherhood of Breath. With its powerful rhythm section and eight-man brass line-up, it was right up his street; he fitted in as soon as he put his horn to his lips.

Intrigued, I had gone to hear the band perform at the 100 Club, a club that had opened the year I was born. I stood listening as the dozen or so musicians—white, black, and in between—played hard over the Sun Ra-Ellington-Dollar Brand chords that Chris McGregor, the band leader, set down. He was a big man with a pointed beard and an African tribal skull cap and sat at the piano like a wizard from *Lord of the Rings*, stoically observing the near chaos of the music, as if he were conjuring it all up to see what would happen. I stood watching and listening, rapt, and envious, knowing I would never be able to play like that.

Chris McGregor, band leader, The Brotherhood of Breath.

The night Gary left with The Brotherhood for tour dates in Germany and Holland, I found a note under my pillow: "Keep playing, baby! You're talented. I love you." I couldn't wait for him to come home, and while I waited, I struggled with the familiar feeling of resentment, at having to cope alone with the boys, the housework, and my piano practice.

One afternoon, not long after he returned home, Chris McGregor and three other South African members of The Brotherhood came over to our flat: Gary's pal, Mongezi Feza, drummer Louis Moholo, and alto sax player Dudu Pukwana. We played one of their irresistibly rhythmic jazz-cum-kwela albums, and while I danced about, one of them rolled a fat joint. Without thinking, I took a couple of totes, and found out the hard way how strong their brand was. I got a bout of palpitations and terrible paranoia, and convinced myself I was insignificant, and without talent. Gary had to sit with me for quite a while to bring me back to my senses.

Now and again that year, Gary went off to play with Centipede. The orchestra had valiantly continued to give performances, and had recorded an album, *Septober Energy*; but for economic reasons, its fifty musicians had been pared down. Gary played with the orchestra at the Royal Albert Hall in October, and again in December, at the Rainbow Theatre, a concert that was intended to be the orchestra's last. The actual last performance would come later, in 1975, at the Lyons Jazz Festival in France.

I don't recall going to either of these prestigious events. It may have had to do with baby-sitting costs, or because I simply didn't feel like going to all his gigs—especially the ones with a big line-up of musicians which I found a bit overwhelming.

This is what Keith and Julie would write about Gary, when I first started a memoir back in 2004: "Gary seemed to explode onto the London jazz scene in the early 1970s. Within a very short time, he was playing with Centipede, The Brotherhood of Breath, Symbiosis, and many splinter groups. He had a wonderful energy and was a force for good: always optimistic, on or off stage, there was never a dull moment. When he returned to America, he was sorely missed. Now that he has passed on, he has left us with so many memories. Everybody loved Gary."

8

We lived now in a constant buzz of creativity. Music, along with the sunlight that poured in from all the windows, filled our spacious flat. On Sunday mornings, we played Coltrane's *A Love Supreme*, or Pharaoh Sanders' *Jewels of Thought*; this was our 'church' music, and despite the anguished notes wrought from their saxophones after beautiful melodic intros, brought peace and reverence into our home.

His appetite for music was insatiable, as if he might die without it. There were always the favorite free-jazz sounds, but now he added rock fusion to the daily playlist. Wayne Shorter's group Weather Report had released their first studio album, *Weather Report* which crossed all musical borders—fusing jazz, R&B, funk and Latin. When Gary brought the Rolling Stones' new *Sticky Fingers* home, although I'd dismissed them up until then, I reveled in the album's blatant raunchiness. There was raunchiness too in J.J. Cale's, "After Midnight...we're going to let it all hang out," and in Captain Beefheart's hoarse 'howlin' wolf vocals.' I was very taken too by The Last Poets, a group of black Americans who were the first hip-hop rappers. Miraculously, in that time of seething black empowerment, their first album sold a million copies.

All this was our daily fare, to which, at the end of that year, I added Carole King's, *Tapestry*. Until then, I hadn't tried to play other artists' songs. But "Natural Woman" resonated so strongly with my own sentiments that I spent hours trying to play it. It was the same with Joni Mitchell, whose album *Blue* echoed through the flat, and became my daily mantra: "I could drink a case of you..."

There are those who only listen to one genre of music, and musicians who only play one genre, perhaps not to dilute themselves, or not to betray the genre they prefer. Neither he nor I were of that ilk; we were both drawn to both ends of the spectrum, and to everything in between. The 1970s' decade was one of musical explosion, one in which jazz, blues, rock, R&B, even folk and country were everywhere overlapping and fusing.

We had been lucky as children to have grown up knowing freedom and peace; we were lucky now to be living in such electrifying musical times.

At this point, I am finding it hard to distinguish between the things that were happening to him and those I was experiencing. We both thrived on all the new ideas, bouncing them back and forth between us, exhilarated with the feeling of nonconformity that came with saying and doing what we felt and believed.

Every day, the music flowed into me, a great pleasure, the soaring imagination, the fire in the belly of the best musicians in the world. Beneath the pleasure, it terrified me too. I wanted so much to cross the divide between listener and player, to create intoxicating sounds with other musicians. I wondered how my muse, Alice Coltrane, had managed, as wife and mother. She was by then experimenting with 'Eastern' and Arabic music, on *Universal Consciousness*, and the familiar tones and rhythms nourished and encouraged my desire to play. So far, there hadn't been a moment when I'd considered giving up. Whatever it was—a life imperative—I couldn't stop playing.

Gary practiced ceaselessly. Each morning, before he began, he had a ritual; a daily discipline. He would sweep and wash the white tiled floors of the flat in his underpants, and then, after taking a shower, still barefoot and wearing on the underpants, would pick up his saxophone, rest it against his bare chest, and start blowing. Nothing about him was conventionally sexy but he had a natural and charismatic sexiness. He would wander from room to room for hours, playing riffs against the walls, to hear different acoustics. Sometimes he'd have a session of circular breathing, and I'd see him standing stock still as he concentrated on keeping notes going, using air he held in his cheeks.

"I'll get it!" I would call out when there was a knock at the door, running to try to beat him to it, to save the visitor from embarrassment at seeing a half-naked man. "It's my home. I'm decent," he'd say, between bursts of voice-like notes, when he'd got there first, and had opened the door to the milkman or a neighbor. Over the years, our lodgers, who were often women, seemed not to be embarrassed because he wasn't embarrassed himself.

◆

I have tried to keep writing chronologically, but am finding it almost impossible to keep up. The memories are like the pieces of an endless jig-saw puzzle: there in my mind, in disorder, not set out neatly to fit into the spaces of consecutive years. I fit a whole section together, and then am stumped by another that doesn't seem to fit.

I do recall that 1972 was the year of the terrorist bombing at the Munich Olympics, of the IRA's Bloody Sunday, and the start of the U.S. Watergate scandal.

At home, after what had seemed like non-stop 'happenings' and drastic changes for the past two or three years, family life settled somewhat, though it could never be called a routine.

On the world music front, Gary was playing guest gigs a lot with Ray Russell, and had a go at forming his own band, the Gary Windo Quartet that included Ray and his drummer, Alan Rushton. I remember he managed to get a couple of gigs for it, and took it to Wales. Jef Langford of *Jazz Journal* wrote: "the forty minutes or so set the scene with both its flaying intensity and warmth of feeling."

Gary playing with Ray Russell's Quartet.

It was in that year that Helen Reddy released "I am Woman," the song that instantly became a rallying-cry for women all over the world. Although it was not the kind of music I would normally have listened to, and my feelings about women's issues had not yet reached boiling point—and despite not having sung for years—I couldn't stop myself yelling out when it came to the chorus: "I am woman. Hear me roar...I can face anything. I am strong, I am invincible, I am woman."

By the following year, 1973, to the world's relief, the most memorable news came when President Nixon finally signed a ceasefire of the United States' bombing of Vietnam.

On the music front, Herbie Hancock's new jazz funk album *Headhunters*, with its hit "Chameleon," took first place on our turntable, with John McLaughlin and Carlos Santana's jazz-fusion tribute to John Coltrane, *Love, Devotion, Surrender*, a close tie.

We were also 'digging' Bob Marley's *Catch a Fire* album. Reggae had been around since the late Sixties, with Jimmy Cliff, Desmond Dekker, and Toots and the Maytals. But now, with Bob Marley and the Wailers, it had become a powerful social and political force, let alone being the hottest dance music around.

Between all the music filling my ears, I found moments of quiet time for reading. I caught up on Germaine Greer's *The Female Eunuch*; and Arthur Janov's *Primal Scream* (I'd always thought it would be amazing to go somewhere far away and scream as loudly as I could!). I even checked out Wilhelm Reich's writings—he thought the world would be a better place if everyone experienced satisfying orgasms. In England, Reich was seen as a crank, but in America, JD Salinger, Saul Bellow and Norman Mailer were all devotees.

Both Gary and I were hooked on Carlos Castaneda's books, beginning with *Journey to Ixtlan*, and were equally intrigued by alternate realities and the power of the spirit, though neither of us had any desire to try mushrooms or mescaline in this cause.

During the spring and summer of 1973, after playing at the prestigious Queen Elizabeth Hall with The Brotherhood of Breath, Gary was working with Robert on another group with a spacey jazz concept—WMWM, an acronym for Wyatt, McRae (Dave), Windo, Matthewson (Ron). They performed a couple of BBC live sessions and were about to record an album when something shocking brought the group to a standstill. We got a call from a friend who was at a party held by poetess Lady June—a party we'd been invited to but for some reason did not go—to tell us that Robert had just fallen from the bathroom window of the fourth floor flat and had broken his back.

Within a day or two, we visited him in Stoke Mandeville hospital where his very shaken-up girlfriend, Alfreda Benge, told us that the doctor had said if Robert hadn't been drunk, he would have died. Asking why he had seen fit to climb out the window, in this terrible aftermath, seemed irrelevant. It was hard to look at him, lying motionless on the starched white sheets, his body wracked with pain, his face gray. I couldn't imagine how as a drummer he would deal with being paralyzed and make a new life.

Julie Christie was there that day too, sitting anxiously by the bed, comforting Alfreda, with whom she'd made friends in Venice during the filming of *Don't Look Now*. The only moment of humor came when Julie called Alfie—Robert's nickname for her—'Gloria Gloom.' It was a sober nature and aloofness rather than gloom, and when I later got to know Alfie, who was a fine artist, I would often see a smile curl at her lips. I liked to think she and I had a tacit understanding: we both lived with talented but crazy musicians and were a bit mad ourselves. My observation was borne out in the lyrics Robert later wrote on "Sea Song," "... Your madness fits in nicely with my own."

A month or so later, Robert would lead us down the hospital hallway, whizzing along in his new wheelchair, to a room with a piano in it. "I get to sneak away for a few hours every day," he said, with a big smile, and then began to pick out a melody.

◆

On what I recall being a very cold day in February, 1974, we headed *en famille* to Wiltshire. Robert was installed in friend Delfina's farmhouse to record the songs he'd written in hospital. Pink Floyd's drummer, Nick Mason, was producing. I was hoping to meet him but by the time we arrived he'd been called away on business.

The farmhouse was cozy, its rooms filled with microphones and instruments and lines leading outside to Virgin's mobile recording studio. Robert was working with the engineer from his wheelchair. I remember his legs went into a spasm of uncontrollable shaking. Seeing us all embarrassed, not knowing what to do, he put his hands firmly on his legs to hold them down and said: "It's nothing. You see, I've had this awful accident," which allowed us all to laugh with him instead of cry.

His plight was a sobering testament to perseverance. Gary was not one for self-pity either; between the two of them, I acquired a disdain of self-pity that has stayed with me all my life.

Over the next few days, I was privy to many magical moments as one by one the musicians recorded their parts on the songs. Some, not surprisingly, were deeply melancholy; others were dreamy, and some, quirky and humorous. I was there when Gary recorded the tortured solo on the track called "Alife." But the unusual circumstances and location had a strong effect on all the musicians: the sounds and style they forged were unique, as yet unheard of.

9

It was in June of 1974 that the IRA, continuing their mainland terrorist campaign, set a bomb in the Houses of Parliament. A month or so later that summer, we went to Tunisia. Gary had accepted the job of band-leader for Doris Troy, a black American soul singer. It was a decision he'd made because he was more worried than usual about finances: England was in a deep recession, with unemployment rampant, causing a period of strikes and riots all over the country. The post-warm boom had officially ended and with it the cuts in arts-funding made by Margaret Thatcher (as Secretary of State for Education and Science) were having a disastrous effect on the number of bookings and venues.

Gary had his own take on being an out-of-work musician, as he explained in an interview in the New Musical Express. The accompanying photo had him comically shrugging, wearing the green and white woolly hat I'd knitted for him. He was reported as saying that that month he'd only taken home to his wife and kids just twelve pounds. Where most other musicians were ashamed to spell out what it was like to be penniless, he felt no such inhibition. He felt that part of the lack of gigs was due to the public having become disillusioned with the word 'jazz.'

He went on: "This scarcity of work has brought about a sort of secrecy among musicians...because they're really afraid that someone will come along and snatch it away from them."

The other reason he took the job with Doris, I suspected, was because she reminded him of his years playing R&B in the U.S.

Doris was the daughter of a Pentecostal minister and had started as a gospel singer in the Bronx. She'd moved on to R&B, and then to pop and rock. When she got a #2 hit in the U.K. with The Hollies' version of "Just One Look," a song she co-wrote, she promptly moved across the Atlantic. Her powerful voice got her gigs as back-up for Dusty Springfield and the Rolling Stones, and on Pink Floyd's *Dark Side of the Moon*. George Harrison became interested too, and signed her to Apple Records, to record an album in her name, on which he and Ringo and other rock luminaries played but which never saw the light of day.

By the time Doris came across Gary, things weren't going so well for her. I sensed I was witnessing the desperate falling from grace, along with Gary's urge to help pick up the pieces. I went to check the band out at Ronnie Scott's, on what happened to be my elder son's birthday.

By then, the boys had come with us to Ronnie Scott's many times. We had walked them right in the door the first time; Pete King had turned a blind eye, and that was that. They saw going there in the evening as an adventure, because it meant a pre-show lamb kebab pita sandwich from a nearby Lebanese café. They knew how to behave and sat with us in the darkened club, fascinated to see their step-father, or other bands we'd gone to hear, playing under the brilliant stage lights. When they got sleepy, we'd tuck them up in the Camper which we parked outside the club. These family outings always made me wish I'd seen my own father when he'd played on stage. Once, after Dizzy Gillespie had played a set, Gary took them over to say hello and shake hands with him.

That night, in the middle of a robust rendering of "When the Saints Go Marching In," Doris caught sight of the boys and raised her arms, calling out, as if in a healing ritual: "Come on up on stage, fellas!" The boys climbed up beside her very large person at which moment, she broke out into "Happy Birthday to you..."

A few months went by during which I remember we spent many evenings at her flat which always seemed to be in darkness, but with plenty of Pall Mall cigarettes and Coca-Cola and Kentucky Fried Chicken handy. American Soul singer Madeline Bell, who was then with top of the charts band, Blue Mink, would often be there, keeping company with Doris.

It was quite by chance that one day I found an article about a music festival in Tabarka, a coral-fishing village in the north of Tunisia, and came up with the idea to try to book Doris' band. It would kill three birds with one stone: it would be work for Gary and the band, an excuse to go back to the country I'd loved, and to show it to my husband.

Ms Troy thought me slightly mad; Gary thought it a great idea and said, "Go for it!" which entailed my going to Paris to see the promoter. Robert contacted his brother, who invited me to stay over. The promoter agreed to meet me, but said he'd already booked the Tunisia acts.

"But Doris fits in with your world music theme," I insisted.

"Oui, but we 'ave already got Country Joe and ze Fish," the promoter said.

With the same blend of naiveté and composure I'd used with the rental agent, I managed to convince the promoter to change his mind. I did wonder for a moment what Country Joe would think when they got the cancelation.

I would have liked to take the boys to Tunisia, but it wasn't possible. At the time, the spare room was rented to a young artist whose canvases—spread across the white floor—looked a lot like Jackson Pollock's work. Andrew was kind and intelligent and seemed responsible. When I asked the boys how they felt about staying with him, they said they'd be fine and did not seem at all concerned that their parents were going to North Africa. Africa was a continent on the page of a school atlas; and at their age, a thousand miles was meaningless.

We arrived in Tunisia in July when the country was an oven. A few days before the festival began, on a scorching dry afternoon, we were sitting in the shade of canvas tents, when there was a great spontaneous jam of African drummers, their beats reverberating for miles into the parched hills and out over the Mediterranean.

Gary could not miss such an opportunity. He got up, put the mouthpiece to his lips and broke into a powerful blues that hung hauntingly over the pounding drums. My body had not forgotten the African rhythms; I got up and danced. Slowly, it was no longer players and audience but a throng of dark sweating bodies, as everyone moved forward and around us in a huge engulfing circle, closing in, clapping and dancing and singing. It was so powerful that we were no longer separate individuals but a nameless tribe. Nigerian drummer Babatunde Olatunji said: "Where I come from, we say that rhythm is the soul of life, because the whole universe revolves around rhythm, and when we get out of rhythm, that's when we get into trouble."

After this spontaneous eruption of desert music, the band's scheduled performance was an anti-climax, and, at least to me—and surely to Gary—a let-down. The band moved on down the coast to play at Hammamet, the beach resort where I'd spent many summer nights dancing with my lover, and then on south for another two hundred miles, to the idyllic island of Djerba, and to another performance at another tourist resort.

Seeing so much of the country again was a thrill, and we had a lot of good times with the band members. But the end of the tour was a disaster. As I'd made the bookings, I was due for a cut of the gig money. In my eagerness, I'd omitted to ask Doris for a contract; which in retrospect, may or may not have made any difference. Speaking for Ms Troy, her bodyguard-boyfriend refused to pay me, and included Gary in this embargo. Even worse, when we arrived at the airport, ready to leave, the event planner had not paid for return air transport for the sound equipment. Doris yelled a lot, took the band on with her, and left us behind to handle it. We were stranded in Tunisia, with almost no money, and only our wits to save us.

My Tunisian lover had not come to see me during our travels because I was now married. The desperate phone call I made to him broke down his pride. Within an hour, and with great relief, we were told that the air transport had now been arranged. When I called to ask how he'd managed to get the planner to pay up, he said he'd threatened him; what exactly he had threatened him with, he wouldn't say.

We had a grueling trip on, via Paris, to Ghent in Belgium, for a last gig, with the two of us handling all the heavy equipment. It was a penance I vowed never to repeat.

Shortly after we had returned home, Doris flew back to the United States, without so much as a call, let alone a check. It was another lesson in paying dues. Neither he nor I dwelled too long on this flagrant injustice. He had seen my Tunisia and there had been some great music. We were both too busy and too enthusiastic about our next plans to let someone else's desperation ruin it all.

The boys had been fine in our live-in artist's care. I was living a life that meant being as daring as a mother as a musician. I didn't compare myself with other mothers, but followed my instinct. As a musician, too, I had to be endlessly resourceful; get knocked over and pick myself up again. Had I been asked if I wanted to change my life—for wealth, security, and comfort—I would without any doubt have said 'no.'

✦

Not long after our North African saga, on September 8, 1974, I was sitting in the audience in the Theatre Royal Drury Lane, waiting for the start of a one-off performance by Robert Wyatt and Friends. The lights went down and the BBC's John Peel walked on stage to introduce the concert.

Among a long and celebrated list of musicians appearing that night were Pink Floyd's Nick Mason, and Mike Oldfield, whose New Age *Tubular Bells* had sold fifteen million copies and launched Richard Branson's Virgin Records. Fringe musician-poet Ivor Cutler was there too. I'd seen him perform several times before. He cut an eccentric figure in his pill-box hat, wrestling with his harmonium while he recited ditties in a lilting Scottish accent. Julie Tippetts performed *a cappella*, "Mind of a Child," one of her own songs. I had gotten to know her better by then and admired how she'd transformed herself: she stood now, looking medieval, in a simple long black dress, without a scrap of make-up. And when Gary stepped forward for his solo on "Alife," I couldn't stop the tears: knowing all the blood, sweat, and tears that had gone into his performance.

But it was Robert who was the star that night; the vulnerability in his voice drew the audience in. In his piercingly sensitive voice, he ended the show with his touching version of The Monkees' hit, "I'm a Believer."

Trying to get backstage after the show was the usual humiliating challenge. I ask myself now why I describe it as humiliating. I simply wanted to get next to my husband, not next to a celebrity. When I found him, he was surrounded by fans showering him with praise and questions. I waited while he mopped himself off and got dressed. When he was ready, he leaned over and said: "We're going on to a party." Neither of us was too keen on parties but he seemed keen to go to this one so I trusted his judgment.

Outside, in the dark streets around Covent Garden, we walked behind a couple of long-haired men in jeans who I assumed were hosting the party. The men stopped beside a BMW and got in the front, and then we got in the back.

As we drove off, I made a sign to Gary to ask who the men were. Formal introductions weren't done in rock circles. "Pink Floyd," he mouthed back; indicating that it was Nick Mason driving and Rick Wright in the passenger seat. It was dark, so I couldn't see the men's faces but I listened as they all agreed it had been a brilliant event. As for where the party was, whether I got to speak with Nick or Rick, or who else was there that night, despite normally having a good memory, I have no recollection whatsoever.

During those first years my husband got to play with the whole gamut of musicians in London, both famous and on the fringe. What intrigued him most was innovative technique and ideas; he lived too fiercely in the present to be concerned about fame and fortune. "I like people who aren't necessarily musicians, who don't go around talking about music all the time… Some of the most boring people I know are musicians. Nothing's worse than spending an evening with name-dropping," he once told a music reporter. "…I think of myself more like a folk musician," he went on. "I play music for folks."

On stage, he simply continued his everyday life, relaxed, yet still the consummate entertainer, a knack that had come from being on stage since his childhood, and from circumstances in which he had learned to entertain himself. I watched him many times, quietly stealing the limelight with casual gestures and comedic expressions, depending on which band he was performing with. Aware he wasn't a typically good-looking man, he hammed it up, wearing a cream golfing cap and a rainbow-colored tank top that displayed his brawny chest and arms.

I borrowed from his persistence and watched his satisfaction with his daily successes, and became more resolute about my own practice, going whenever possible into semi-seclusion—"in the cupboard," he would joke. Although his prowess was a constant reminder of my own lack, he was in fact my inspiration, my 'main man.'

As well as tenor saxophone, he played alto saxophone and flute because a saxophone session man was expected to play all those instruments, although he never troubled himself to master them. After his saxophone, the apple of his eye was the bass clarinet of African Blackwood that he had treated himself to, and with whose deep mellow tones, and *Tune a Day on Bass Clarinet*, he experimented for hours.

◆

The music room was, ironically, next to the kitchen. I spent hours in the sound-proofed room, experiencing splendid moments of accomplishment as well as agonizing rages and depressions. I would go back and forth between the piano and the stove, and there were many times I'd smell something burning when it was already too late; too lost in sounds to notice smells. I once boiled a kettle down to a solid lump of aluminum. I still enjoyed cooking, but was becoming increasingly disenchanted with the idea of housework in general, partly because it took time away from music, and partly because of the humdrum image I felt it gave me.

Sometimes during a practice session, I would shout like a tortured prisoner at a mistake I'd made and he would come rushing in to pacify me. More than once, I thumped so hard, I broke a key. "It's kinda normal to beat up your axe," he joked, as he fixed it. He was most endearing when he put me back together after one of these anxiety attacks. With me, he had the patience of Job.

I remember one evening vividly when he was out at a gig. I bought a pint of whiskey at the off-license and drank it all. My fits of despair were a hellish concoction of jealousy, about the women he might be meeting, and my slow progress as a musician. When he came home, he found me lying on the bed fully clothed, my face stained with tears and black eye-liner. He picked up the bottle. "Hey Baby! What are you doing?" he asked. "Just keep playing. You're doing fine." And then to cheer me up, "Lots of musicians are self-taught and just do things their own way."

He and I complemented each other; we knew that. He was helping me break through creative barriers and taboos while I was giving him a home and the affection of a family. "We're supposed to be together, you know that, right?" he said.

◆

Always on the look-out for places to sit in to keep the musical juices flowing, he discovered *Peanuts*. It was known for its Friday-night jam sessions for which all the free-blowing jazz musicians in London, as well as those visiting from Europe, showed up. "This small club above a London pub (the King's Arms) behind Liverpool Street station was the place of so much fantastic music. Every Friday night something would happen. I played there many, many times." I discovered this, handwritten by Gary, when I was sorting through a pile of cuttings.

I was nowhere near ready to sit in, but it was a good place to get an idea of what that meant, with one musician after the other arriving and moving forward to be a part of the *melée*. One night, friend Marc Charig was blowing his trumpet full steam ahead with the power duo, drummer Louis Moholo and bassist Harry Miller, when his hair caught on fire from a candle blazing on a metal stand. Before anyone in the audience moved, I rushed at him and somehow patted the flames out. Marc swiveled round, still blowing his trumpet, and stared at me as if I'd gone berserk. I pointed to the candle and then at his hair at which he merely shrugged and carried on playing.

Gradually, in the anonymity of the music room, I found myself letting go more, with a mixture of the chords I'd mastered and free improvisation. Gary would sometimes come in to play along, and make it a duo.

And then there were the impromptu home-grown jam

sessions. Laurie Allan, a minimalist drummer, was one of the first musicians I jammed with. A slim and reticent man, he was not one of the 'heavies' on the scene but had played with John McLaughlin and would go on to drum with Daevid Allen's psychedelic fusion-rock band Gong. I felt nervous, but I liked him. And it helped that Gary neither made excuses for my being there, nor instructed me on how or what to play. He knew I would never be a virtuoso, and yet he encouraged me; perhaps simply because of something he had heard in my playing.

Jumping right in on that first session I set down a couple of chords in a basic rhythm. Laurie took up the groove and then Gary blew over us. We played free of time or melody, and without getting high, listened carefully to each other and creating a spontaneous and unique conversation. The process was like a moving sculpture: hewing shapes from raw material, which was sound itself. Gary recorded the session on a four-track reel-to-reel perched atop my piano, to listen back to, to enjoy, and learn from.

Some thirty years later, the recorded session would be released on an album produced by avant-garde jazz buff Michael King. When I heard it, it felt as if I were listening to someone else.

Slowly, with certain musicians, I became a bona fide member of the clan. Frank Perry was next to come and jam with us. Frank was a percussionist *extraordinaire*, a pioneer of New Age music long before it was called that. He was one of the most serious-minded musicians I'd met; jokes were rare, his musical vision was his life's work. After playing in several groups, including Ovary Lodge, he had by then bravely embarked on a solo career. His kit was so complex it took him two hours to assemble in the music room—all kinds of Tibetan gongs, shells, bells and cymbals, the sounds of which he used as spiritual healing. Sitting at my piano, the kit was so large and dense I couldn't see him behind it, and it gave the impression it was playing itself. The session with Frank was also recorded, and would be included on the same album as the one with Laurie Allan. "Perry's extended percussive palette lends the music an expansive air..." Nic Jones will write later write, in *All About Jazz*.

Somehow, Gary managed to entice Frank to join us when we gave a class in free improvisation at the boys' school. After we performed, we gave percussion instruments to the children—tambourines, cymbals, castanets, triangles—and told them they could play whatever they wanted. After they got over their bewilderment at the idea they could do this in the presence of adults, they lost all inhibition and created a truly liberating cacophony.

When the hullabaloo had ended, and we were packing up, a boy came over to me, "Are you David Bowie?" he asked. It wasn't long after Bowie's *Ziggy Stardust* album. I was skinny, lined my eyes with kohl and had dyed my spiky short hair with red henna.

"No. I'm a lady," I replied, tickled with the compliment.

◆

He had become accustomed to, and enjoyed, going on the road—especially in Europe, where British avant-garde jazz groups were in such great demand, the musicians had become legendary. He always came home with stories of high-jinks and pranks; in hotels and on airplanes. One stood out; another saxophone player had casually asked a passing air stewardess: "Any chance of a fuck?"

His absences were always a wrench and though I enjoyed hearing about the performances, the reviews, and the stories, they brought up the burning issue of infidelity. I'd been to enough clubs to know that wherever there were musicians, there were women eager to get close to them. Performers have built-in powers of seduction. And I understood, reluctantly, that it was a great temptation. Having played his heart out, especially on the road, why would he resist the advances of an attractive woman?

He didn't resist. One night, he didn't come home. In the early hours of the morning, after pacing the hall, I picked up the phone and called the house in Islington where musicians hung out. I asked for him, and he came to the phone. Before he could say anything, I asked, "Why didn't you come home? Are you with a woman?"

His voice came low over the phone, "Yes. I'm here with someone."

I remember yelling, "How could you?" I had asked for the truth, but wasn't prepared to hear it.

And then, after a brief pause, knowing what he was about to say would provoke an outburst, he went on: "Maybe I shouldn't come home? I can't really say it won't happen again." He was serious. It was a preposterous notion, and it took my breath away.

I was bent double, with the phone clasped against my ear, and saw my life stretch out before me, without him. From somewhere, came the words, "I want you to come back." It had been the make-or-break moment. When someone knows who he is and what he wants, and has the courage to tell you, it leaves you free to decide.

While I waited for him to come home, I went over what had happened. He hadn't said the words, 'open marriage,' but that is what he meant. It was part of the Hippie credo of free love and the uninhibited expression of all feelings. I had left my first marriage because I had committed adultery, and until this moment, the one-man-at-a-time model had been ingrained in me. He had faced me with infidelity, and with staying instead of leaving. I could stop here, or go on.

It all echoed back: my Bohemian had spoken of Jean-Paul Sartre and Simone de Beauvoir, and their pact to maintain their 'essential love,' and to have 'contingent lovers.' I had recently become more involved in the feminist movement's doctrines, the main one being that women should demand more honesty and openness from men. I had done just that, and he had been honest. It was more than a 'personal' moment. In that hectic time of 'waking up' but not knowing how to achieve what men had already achieved, it was to men who were 'someone,' who were doing something exciting and could offer more than a lifetime of financial security, that women were attracted. And I was no exception.

He came in looking disheveled and tired, and put down his horn case. He was quieter and more somber than usual. I was exhausted, in a state of shock. But I pelted him with questions. Sexual attraction defies explanation, I knew that. But I couldn't stop myself wanting to understand what had attracted him to her, and what she knew and did, that I didn't.

He seemed to want to both comfort me and stand his ground. I shouted a lot, and he absorbed it all. And then he said, "I love you. You know I do. But you can be free, too, and do what you want. What's wrong with making love to someone else sometimes?"

A month later, after broaching the idea with me first, he brought the woman home. It had been a one-night stand, but she was back in town and he'd seen her at a club. To my astonishment, he said, "She likes women too."

It was about the time that hot pants were the craze. When she arrived at the flat, we were both wearing them, along with towering wedge-heeled sandals. Apart from these, physically, we were opposites. She was statuesque in height, with big matronly breasts, white skin, jet-black hair cut very short, and a good deal of eye make-up.

A few glasses of wine dissolved the last barriers of properness, and from a shared bubble bath in which her breasts floated like balloons, we listened to the bluesy riffs Gary was playing for our benefit in the hall. When he brought us refills of wine, we splashed him, which brought the boys in to see what the commotion was about. As it resembled their own bath-time, they smirked and went off to play again.

After dinner we smoked the joint she rolled, I put on J.J. Cale, and the three of us settled on the mattresses. Gary stood back to let whatever was going to happen, happen. He knew to let her lead, and was smiling to see the surprise and pleasure on my face. That night, in a maternal-sisterly manner, she gave me a late-comer's initiation into a love in. To his male eagerness and impatience, she added the female touch, gently opening up sex to 'the other,' in this case, another woman.

After this, I embarked on my first 'infidelity,' which wasn't now an infidelity. I seduced a man I met at a neighbor's house; that he was married too didn't deter either of us. It was, for me, if not for him, an urgent but token ritual that marked the end of another sort of virginity.

I told Gary about my first fling to let him know the open marriage he wanted was now official. I felt the high of seizing the moment, and being the one in control of sex, as if the kind of carnal knowledge men were privy to might lead to deeper creativity. Women's lib and the Hippies' 'make love not war' justified any misgivings I felt about promiscuity. The jolt to my libido flowed into my music. I shut myself away to practice for hours, perhaps partly in penance.

Having got a taste of free love, I let myself continue as and when it took my fancy. The men seemed bemused, sometimes struck dumb, but like men everywhere, took advantage of this new phenomenon: the sexually-liberated, i.e., sexually-available, woman. I was flattered by the attentions and the compliments: one lover said *"I just had to touch you."* Another admitted he had not made the first move because he thought me 'untouchable,' meaning I was married.

As a couple, we also entertained an occasional ménage à trois. I saw these as the Hippie version of the wife-swapping that was going on in the suburbs; though it's unlikely my ex-husband and I would ever have indulged in these.

All this did nothing to stop my jealousy about his flings.

I would plague him with questions when I knew of or suspected an affair—and I certainly suspected more than there actually were. He would answer, at first briefly, trying to avoid the truth and the subsequent scene, and then reluctantly tell me more, to put an end to the questions.

On the other hand, when I had a fling, all he would ask was, "So was it good?" Since we shared everything else, to punish him for his own dalliances, I would give him a few tantalizing details. If he ever regretted being the author of our open marriage, he never showed it. He either hid whatever discomfort he felt about my affairs, or refused to think about them. In *The Marriage of Heaven and Hell*, William Blake wrote: "The path of excess leads to the palace of wisdom." And this too: "Without Contraries is no progression. Attraction and Repulsion, Reason and Energy, Love and Hate, are necessary to Human existence."

This all brings up the issue of AIDS, which had not yet started its devastating world-wide rampage. Oblivious of what was to come, we simply permitted ourselves to enjoy this unprecedented sexual freedom from judgment or repercussions.

Condoms were what our parents had used for family planning, and were too unappealing for the climate of free love and flower power.

I had stopped using the pill but did not stop to wonder why I didn't get pregnant. Nor did either of us ever bring up the subject. My two sons were more than enough for me, for us both. I was fortunate too, not to get pregnant by one of my lovers.

I must write all this, despite the fact it sometimes portrays the man I knew and loved in a somewhat darker light. His life had made him his own person. He owned his past, his sins and strengths, and his weaknesses. I want most to bring to life how he was both an easy man to live with—he didn't sweat the little things, or judge, or criticize—and a hard taskmaster, who insisted on living life to the fullest. He was both of his time and ahead of it. And perhaps the most valuable thing he taught me was living with opposites. "I have tried, however unsuccessfully, to live again the follies and sentimentalities and exaggerations of the distant time, and to feel them, as I felt them then, without irony."—Graham Greene.

    I have written about the boy and the man I knew, about the musician and the father. As a husband, he looked after me well; in sickness and in health, he watched over me, and I wanted for little. As a lover, he was eager, adventurous, and generous, always spontaneous, never predictable. There was a fire and urgent curiosity about our lovemaking and I wonder now if some of that passion, on my side, was not spurred on by my imaginings about the other women he made love to. Jealousy is also an aphrodisiac. I took to reading Erica Jong's *Fear of Flying*. "Jealousy is all the fun you think they had," she wrote. Her book was my validation for what she called the "zipless fuck"—having great sex with a man you didn't know, and, would never know.

10

Musically, I was moving along, if slowly. But there were times now when Gary would come bursting into the music room, insisting: "Play that again!" And then he'd join in, and we'd lose ourselves playing. We were developing our own special musical intimacy. "I love listening to you play," he said, with satisfaction. I suppose I was his protégé.

But the better I got, the more time I longed for, to practice. I was constantly taking stock of the scene, watching out for women jazz musicians to appear, especially jazz pianists. Marian McPartland would not become known until 1978, after she had left England and was hosting a jazz radio program in America. But there were as yet no women visibly breaking new ground in England. There were women jazz vocalists—Cleo Laine, Blossom Dearie and Maggie Nichols—whom I went to hear whenever possible. And of course, there were all those women musicians playing or singing in a jazz band or group, in local halls or pubs, without ever being known to a larger public.

With time now so important, I began to rail at anything that seemed to unfairly take me away from practicing. I remember with shame one particular evening, when, instead of cooking dinner, I went to get us hamburgers at a new place in Hampstead.

As I stood waiting in a long queue, I worked myself into a stew of self-pity, thinking of my husband at home practicing.

When I finally got back home, and opened the front door and called out, no one appeared to claim their dinner. The smooth notes of a saxophone and the yells of my sons went on over my voice. In a fit of pique, I threw the large box of hamburgers down the hall, shouting, as it slid along the floor, "Here's dinner. Come and get it!"

The saxophone notes stopped, as did the boys' shouting, and when the three of them converged in the hall, there was a stunned silence as they saw their supper spread out on the floor. The only redeeming factor was that the floor, thanks to Gary's daily efforts, was clean. Mortified, I watched the three of them retrieve the hamburgers and set off to the kitchen for plates.

Another of my outbursts involved alto-sax player Elton Dean. Elton had been a member of Soft Machine, and was well-known in the jazz scene. He had been in a band called Bluesology with Reggie Dwight, who would later borrow Elton's first name—along with John, from Long John Baldry (who like him, was gay)—to make his stage name, Elton John.

Elton came over one morning to chat with Gary about a new group. Not one for pleasantries, Elton made the mistake of barely acknowledging my presence—and not for the first time. When the two men went downstairs to the tradesmen's drive, where Gary had work to do on the Camper, still indignant about being ignored, I filled a bucket with water, went to the kitchen window and aiming at Elton, chucked it down.

"Jesus Christ!" Elton yelled, looking up, his long hair wet and bedraggled. When the two of them came upstairs, Gary handed his friend a towel but said nothing; perhaps relishing it as a scene from a cartoon or comedy show.

These scenes were the result of being split in two, or rather in three: between enjoying being a mother and wife, but seeing them as perpetually restricting, and the battle to express my ideas in the company of all the male musicians I was meeting.

I had by then discovered Valerie Solanas and her *SCUM Manifesto* (Society for Cutting up Men). When I had still been living in suburban cotton wool, Valerie had shot that great misogynist Andy Warhol, almost killing him. She did it, she said, because Warhol had been messing her around about a play she'd written and given him, bluntly entitled Up Your Ass. Men, she said, were incomplete women, missing chromosomes, and therefore inferior not superior to women. In her ravings, she even proposed gender-cide. I was drawn by the idea that a woman had been driven to this extreme.

A few weeks later, we were invited to a party at Elton's place. He walked up to us with a smile and a glass of red wine in his hand. With a nonchalant flourish, he tipped the wine all over my blouse. And that seemed to be the end of it. Water and wine are safer than bullets.

Valerie Solanas would die homeless, aged fifty-two, of madness and pneumonia, never knowing her manifesto would remain in bookstores for years to come; that a movie of her life, *I Shot Andy Warhol*, would be made in 1996, and that her play would be posthumously produced in 2000.

◆

My affairs continued and I enjoyed every one—each was a conquest on my part: because I was married, it was up to me to make the first move. That I was simply emulating what men did, or wanted to do, didn't occur to me: whatever the impulse, by then, I would have found it hard to give up.

He was as accommodating as ever, though I sensed odd moments when he bit his tongue. Although I knew he wasn't attracted to a woman just for sex, but because she was interesting and intelligent, my jealousy was like a fever, barely controllable.

My belief that the sexual act was the most intimate thing a man and woman could do had been superseded. It occurs to me as I write that had we both been as jealous as I was, none of it would have been possible. We loved each other and drove each other crazy, in different ways, but in equal measure. A normal couple would have called it quits. And somewhere in my conscience, if not in his, was the notion that we'd made it impossible ever to attempt a conventional marriage.

I recall there being several occasions when he'd try to shock me out of my jealous rage. He would pack a bag, grab his saxophone case and walk out the door, refusing my shouts to not leave me. He always came back a few hours later and I would behave as if nothing had happened. Once, when he was about to leave, we wrestled in the hallway, by the front door, until we fell on the tile floor and made love.

My jealousy was never about his popularity or his musical talent. The rivalry I felt—for perhaps it was simply rivalry—was purely sexual.

The writing of all this is an exercise in memory selection, the choosing among an immeasurable number of moment-images. It is also in part an exorcism of the shame I buried at the time, a left-over from Victorian morality, and in part a reflection on all the things I said and did in the name of love and freedom. "Freedom's just another word for nothing left to lose," was the chorus of Kris Kristofferson's unforgettable Hippie hymn, "Me and Bobby McGee."

✦

Gary brought a good deal of humor—and slapstick—into our lives, too. He had survived on humor, and saw himself as a cartoon character: I was Olive Oyl to his Popeye.

From years of watching *The Honeymooners*, The Three Stooges and The Marx Brothers, he had accumulated a repertoire of facial expressions, one-liners, and sound effects. They were things he knew no one dared to say in real life but would love to, and he gave himself the role of spokesman. Most of it was harmless, but sometimes I cringed inwardly at the crudeness of the gags he came out with.

We were after all living in the decade of the great irreverent British comedians—when nothing was sacred. He mimicked the Monty Python sketches: "Look, Matey! I know a dead parrot when I see one. This is an ex parrot," or, "I can't afford a whole new brain."

There was a night we laughed ourselves silly. Elton Dean came over to our flat with a couple of friends and a bootleg of the first of the *Derek and Clive* albums made by Peter Cook and Dudley Moore. British humor was already rife with self-parody; now, obscenity was added to the mix, with Cook and Moore playing public-toilet attendants in an inane ad-lib dialogue rife with "fuck offs" and "cunts." They'd made the recording as a private joke but the bootleg became so popular the mad duo went on to record two more albums.

Gary reveled in all this mocking of English manners; adlibbing and swearing like a trooper to entertain his fellow musicians during the long hours of waiting backstage before and between performances, and during the tiring hours of travel.

◆

I was way behind the times in trying LSD, especially after his description of how his own trips had gone south. "I was out of my body, watching myself from overhead. And then I got real paranoid. I thought I saw the fuzz outside in the street, waiting to bust me," he said. They weren't there then, but they *were* there later.

Nevertheless, he was the one who suggested it, and I doubt I would have tried it if he hadn't. One sunny Saturday, he squeezed some clear drops of liquid onto cubes of white sugar and we ate them. Instead of sitting around going gaga, we went first to visit friends, which was not one of his better ideas. There, I became paranoid, so he excused us and we set off instead on a 'walk about' in Regent's Park where the ducks on the lake seemed to come at me in 3D, and the water swelled like an ocean. The colors of the sky, grass, and flowers shimmered just as they had in my childhood experiences of nature.

We walked along the banks of Regent's Canal and on up Primrose Hill, with its giddying vistas of London spread out below, and, with my heart racing, talked nonstop about all the exciting changes in our lives, about seeing the truth of things, stuff that, like a dream, disappears on waking. It was only walking with my familiar husband on familiar territory that kept me from falling over the edge of reality and sanity.

After several hours, we made our way home over Hampstead Heath. We cooked supper for the boys and I clearly recall tucking them into bed, feeling like a child myself, as if the rigors of motherhood had dropped away.

We were still high, but he wanted to go to the Country Club where Ginger Baker was showcasing his new group, Baker Gurvitz Army. At the club, I was still in the acid's grip, staring at the bright blur of stage lights, beneath which Ginger's frizzy red hair looked like a huge fiery halo. Ginger had been the drummer with the super group Cream until they'd broken up in 1968. He'd been to Africa since then and was pounding out rhythms that touched a familiar spot in me. I wanted to get up and dance, but Ginger was an icon, and the audience was riveted to their seats by his technique.

Gary was hoping to sit in and went over to speak to Ginger on a break between numbers. When he finally got a nod, he grabbed his horn and stepped onstage, puffing first at his inhaler. He had got into the habit of taking great gulps of air, of life—and the only time he exhaled as deeply was when he played his saxophone.

The music went on into the night. He sat in again and afterwards hung out with the other musicians. I had just about 'come down' by the time we drove home, at the end of a day of 'consciousness-raising' that had seemed to last an eternity.

◆

The Hippie movement was slowly petering out, with much of its fashions and many of its ideas either abandoned or absorbed into the mainstream. In its wake came the full-on Women's Liberation Movement—the second wave of emancipation that had been building since the 1950s, and which had by then been given its less militant tag of 'Women's Lib,' a pun even had it as 'Women's Libido.' As its influence grew, it took a hold on me, especially as I was figuring out how I could become stronger in my life, and more visible in the world.

It was the movement's sexual aspect that most interested me; with its insistence on making demands for men to understand our bodies and our orgasms—how precious and naïve that sounds now. From free love, we were moving on to learning about our bodies. I did as they said and used a mirror to examine all the parts of me. The idea behind this was to refuse to compromise ourselves; meaning, we shouldn't take shit from our men-folk.

I wasn't one to join groups, but was inclined to take action on my own. It must have been about then, on a sudden impulse, I took Gary's razor and chopped off my long hair. Long hair, the feminists said, was a demeaning ploy to please men.

When he saw the crooked crew cut I'd given myself, he applauded, "Wow! You really did it." He may have preferred my long hair, but he would not dampen my elation. Perhaps he saw the action itself as sexy? When I later discarded my bra, he smiled, "I can see your pointy nipples now!" He watched all this female frolicking with delight and the politicking about men's faults with interest rather than affront.

It didn't occur to me or to most women that while we were freeing ourselves from sexual constraints, we were freely giving men what they wanted. One thing led to another: as well as achieving orgasms, we wanted the right to that male stronghold known as ambition. I began to take the new confrontational approach: whatever brought equality and freedom of thought and action was good. Therapists were in vogue to help you apply this self-confrontation and confrontation with others, to help unblock energy and creativity. I didn't go to see one, in part due to lack of money, but mostly because I was a born autodidact... and because Gary almost always got me out of my funk.

◆

There are some people you never forget because they say or do something to hit the spot just when you need it.

Ray Russell was one of those people. One evening, when Gary was away on the road, I went over to see Ray. "For your music, listen to other musicians but don't try to imitate them. Believe in yourself. It will come." And about my worries over Gary, "Yeah, well... There are personalities so wide that those narrower ones get lost in all the space," he said, drawing a diagram to illustrate his point.

As well as words of wisdom, I got a job that evening. I offered to do some roadie-ing for Ray's band: we needed the money and I could make use of the Camper. Despite his insistence that it was too tough a job for a woman, Ray agreed. The first gig worked well enough, with him helping me lift the equipment, and me driving. But the second time, on the way home late at night on the West Way, the Camper broke down. It was a faulty fuel line, and luckily, Gary had shown me how to fix it. I had to roll underneath the chassis and re-connect the line. And with that, my days as a roadie were over.

When I did at last decide to take piano lessons, it was, at Gary's suggestion, Stan Tracey whom I called. Stan was one of the most talented and respected jazz piano players in London at the time, with a style between Duke Ellington and Thelonious Monk. Years later, Stan would receive both an OBE and a CBE for his contributions to British jazz. When Stan agreed to see me, I was almost too scared to go.

I recall sitting on a stool beside him at his upright piano. He was a quiet man and began by asking, "What do you want from me?" It was an anti-climax as I didn't really know what I wanted. I must have explained that I practiced scales and exercises, that I knew some chords, and played a lot of free improvisation, but wanted to get a better grasp on theory.

I was too in awe to take in much of what Stan showed me. By the end of the lesson it must have been as clear to him as it was to me that I was not a candidate for a regular student.

"Don't worry about it," Gary said. "You're doing great as you are. I hear you put chords together that sound really cool. And, you know, so many musicians are self-taught."

◆

One quiet afternoon, a loud and insistent knock at the door warned us of trouble. Gary went to open it as he was, barechested, and wearing jeans. "Yes officers? Come in," I heard him say, obligingly. He led the two men to our bedroom balcony, and pointed at two very small marijuana plants set amongst some pots of geraniums. We had put in a few seeds from a joint one day, mostly as an experiment, and hadn't yet pulled a single leaf. The police must have come on a tip-off, from a neighbor who found our lifestyle too colorful.

I stood in silent panic as the officers packed the plants into a bag and escorted my husband out of the flat, advising me as they did that he was being taken to Hampstead police station. I quickly made a series of calls, the last one to an entertainment solicitor who handled musicians' drug charges, of which there were many in those days. Gary was home in a few hours, free of either a charge or a fine. The boys, fortunately, had been at school.

A year or so later, when we would dare to progress to the risky and expensive purchase of a gram of cocaine—only half of which we had sampled—there would be another brisk knock at the door, and he would again be led away by two detectives. And was again let go, due to the repeat efforts of our solicitor, to whom we were eternally grateful. After that, we forwent the cultivation of marijuana and the purchase of cocaine.

Even without hallucinogens, I went into a season of flying dreams and nightmares. I would feel a sort of wrench in my body as I took off from the bed and rose up to the ceiling, which looked exactly as it did in daytime. There, I would circle round and around for a while, like a witch without a broomstick, feeling the dizzying circling motion, and aware I was doing something that wasn't possible in my waking life.

The nightmares came in the dead of night. I would wake and see a huge black form bending over me, and let out a bloodcurdling scream. I'd throw out my arms to push the form back, and even with my eyes wide open, could still see the dark shape until I came to and it faded. Each time, Gary would jump out of his skin and shout, "Jesus, Pammy! What happened?"

This nightmare continued until we took up karate. It was of course his idea, not mine. He craved a sport in his life. There were two reasons I joined him, the first was the idea of learning self-defense, the other was that karate was a form of dancing. Like all girls, I'd been brought up to fear men's potential violence; without being given any kind of instruction on self-defense. Such things, ironically, were for men only.

We joined a club teaching the Wado-ryu style under the 8th Dan master, Sensei Tatsuo Suzuki. Gary threw himself into it with typical fervor, and I followed keenly, though with slightly less fervor. We jogged on the Heath—sometimes, rashly, barefoot, because he had read that it strengthened the feet—and practiced kicks, aiming at trees. In class, I would catch sight of him: fierce and focused, his wire-rimmed glasses tied around his head with tape so they wouldn't fall off while he was sparring. Twice, as a result of being too pugnacious, he received a bloody nose.

I got roped into going with him to see Bruce Lee movies to keep up the impetus, and it was the time too of the cult TV series Kung Fu with David Carradine, which the whole family was hooked on.

In time, we would both earn brown belts. Years later, now on my own, I would earn the coveted black belt. Looking back, I did so many things I would never have done, out of love for him; and because he loved me. This is from Tahar Ben Jelloun: "When [Miguel] looked back over his life, he saw it as simply a series of stages in which a loving infatuation had often been decisive."

It wasn't long after starting karate that I sent the fearful nightmare monster packing. I dreamed there was a knock at the door and when I went to open it, a huge male form was trying to get in. I pushed against the door as hard as I could, until I managed to close it. After that, the specter never returned. Our karate master used to say, to discourage the wrong use of the techniques: "Let the enemy present himself."

The tough training stimulated physical and mental focus and, in my case, added to my growing self-confidence. My playing progressed as if another part of me had been unlocked.

11

As the year 1975 came upon us, in the grizzly month of February we took the boys and drove down to Oxfordshire. We were going to Richard Branson's brand-new studio, The Manor, where Robert was recording his second album, *Ruth is Stranger than Richard*. Our arrival was greeted by two enormous Irish wolfhounds called Bootleg and Beatrice, who were far too friendly to be considered guard-dogs.

The Manor was causing quite a stir in the recording industry. Away from city distractions, it offered a rural environment where musicians could stay for the duration instead of coming and going each day.

I'd met Richard Branson a few weeks before, when we'd gone to a party at his London flat. With his head of platinum blond hair, and his broad toothsome smile, he wasn't easy to miss as he whirled among his musician and celebrity friends. He was the musician's hero, and at twenty-four, was already a legend. He would have no truck with the idea of a big corporation, but did everything his way, like a cottage industry: going from selling bootleg tapes by mail-order to founding Virgin Records, and, the following year, to opening Virgin Megastores. And ten years after that, he'd inaugurate Virgin Airlines.

During the next few days at The Manor, Gary spent most of the time in the studio, and I'd join him there for an hour or two each day. It was the first time I met bass-player Hugh Hopper, the fourth founding member of Soft Machine, and another bass-player, Bill MacCormick, who'd been in a band called Quiet Sun with Phil Manzanero. Multi-instrumentalist Fred Frith, the founder of Henry Cow, was also there.

I recall coming upon Brian Eno, too, looking serious in his signature blue beret. He was at The Manor to record his own material—*Another Green World*—as well as play synthesizer tracks for Robert. When Gary saw Brian, he made a crunched-up face. It didn't surprise me to see a hint of animosity: there couldn't have been two more different personalities. Gary was an extrovert and a full-on musician, while Brian was an introvert and a self-confessed 'non-musician.' He'd not long left Roxy Music because he'd got bored with the rock star life. I remember thinking that what we saw as standoffishness was a defense—his innovative ideas and idiosyncratic methods weren't as popular then as they would later become.

It didn't occur to me that my own career in music might have proved easier to achieve had I come to the same conclusion as Brian and accepted a 'non-musician' status. Not only was I married to a true musician, and surrounded by them, I'd been brought up like everyone else of my era to believe proficiency was the only way to be successful at anything. Brian and a few other artist-musicians at the time—eccentric as they often were—were proving that the opposite was possible.

◆

On May 24, 1975, for my thirty-third birthday, I found a giant card on my piano. It had a daffodil-yellow background and huge stylized letters—*P A M*—edged in black, blue and red, each filled in with hundreds of minuscule black-ink versions of my name: *Pamela, Pam, Pammy*, with a line of xxx's and, *I love you, from*

Gary, at the bottom. It must have taken hours to make, and I still treasure it.

There were gigs, and one-night bands, and plans and ideas. But he was always so keen to play and to pay the rent—and so ready to help other musicians—that he now jumped at another ill-omened offer. "Necessity acquaints a man with strange bedfellows" was Shakespeare's observation. Or, as Plato wrote: "...necessity is the mother of our invention."

An English singer by the name of Norma Green, who no-one had heard of, had a booking for a two-week residency in Switzerland and needed a band. I don't remember asking Gary how or where he'd met her, but watched him rally together a group of musicians: blues guitarist Rich Brunton who'd been playing with King Crimson's founding member Pete Sinfield; bass-player Clive Griffiths, a member with Mike Patto of Dick and the Firemen; drummer and Richard Gere look-alike David Dowle, and keyboard pla yer Frank Roberts.

As it was the school summer holidays, we took the boys with us, and the bass-player brought his wife and two children. We were eleven in all. The large house we were given for our stay was on a rugged hillside overlooking Lake Lugano. It seemed an idyllic place for a getaway, and we were soon enjoying plenty of swimming and fishing and lolling in the sun by the lake.

But events quickly proved otherwise. After the first night's show, Gary came back with a fixed grin on his face that spelled defeat, "It's a bloody sleazy strip joint!" The next night, I went with the bass-player's wife to see what he meant, and came face to face with a troupe of half-naked girls.

A music critic, surprised to come across Gary in such odd circumstances, wrote: "Ms Green's act contained nothing much to distinguish it from that of countless dolly birds flogging round the nightclub circuit. 'Hello, you groovy cats,' was one of her introductions." The bemused reviewer continued: "The group turned out in some sharp red and blue satin suits seemingly left behind by some musicians used to playing the Butlin's circuit... and were the choice of Ms Green's manager...before and after her appearance, the group played numbers which touched on Sly and the Family Stone, American rock à la Allman Brothers, shades of Herbie Hancock, and some odd Brotherhood riffs, in solos by Gary and Mongezi Feza... If you get a chance, go see them."

After a week or so of this, Gary asked Ms Green to pay the band some wages on account. In a repeat performance of the Doris Troy fiasco, Ms Green's muscle-bound Swiss boyfriend-manager said they'd have to wait. In relating this to the band, Gary's face crumpled; for once, showing pain. "We've done it again!" he blurted out. "There's no gig money." And with that he reached out and grabbed his saxophone, which was leaning against a stone wall. He held it for a moment, and then hurled it back at the wall. I was horrified: the impact dented the bell of the horn and bent some of the keys. It was the first time I'd seen him take out his frustration on his beloved instrument.

He put his broken horn in its case and we consulted with the band members over cups of tea. We were all broke by now, getting by on pancakes and figs from the trees in the garden. He got their spirits up with jokes, "We're British! We're not going to be defeated," and came up with the idea that we should hitch home. Nobody refused or complained. He told the bass player to take his family to the British Consulate to request passage home; they'd have a better chance if all eleven of us didn't show up for help.

It was early morning and the weather was fine. Before we all separated, we took a group photograph on the side of the autobahn, to show the starting line. He was hopeful we'd reach Ostend by late afternoon to catch the last ferry. He put out his thumb with a resigned smile, as if he were saying, *"I know this looks irresponsible with these young children, but please believe me, there's a good reason."* I took turns in putting out my thumb, and we jumped

The starting point for our historic hitch-hike from Lugano back home to London. I am not in the photo because I was the one who took it.

in and out of cars, like a relay race.

One man, the owner of a shiny new Mercedes, took pity on us and treated us to lunch. The last driver, an African-American whose name was Bunny, drove sixty miles out of his way to make sure we reached Ostend in time. My embarrassment, with children in tow, was mitigated by an unexpected reminder of the kindness of strangers.

By then, we had little left in the way of money, for the ferry or food. "Okay," Gary said to my younger son. "Go behind that family and all their suitcases." My son bent low and crept unseen onto the ferry, thus avoiding the ticket collector. "Now we can buy some hamburgers!" he said. His free-thinking made him brazen and adventurous even when we were down and out.

It was a beautiful calm afternoon on the channel. A fellow passenger took a photograph. We are on deck under a perfect blue sky, looking tanned and happy, the epitome of a family on a carefree holiday.

We arrived home late that night and within a day, the others arrived home safely too. We got together and shared our stories. It would be the last flop of its kind. "Fool me twice..."

Not the least bit put off, Gary continued to collect musicians of all kinds. I think it was because he didn't get upset by what people said or thought about him. And though he took his music seriously, he never took himself too seriously.

I too began to branch out. It wasn't that I turned my back on free-form playing, more of a natural progression: as I discovered more chord patterns, melodies would emerge from them. And then words came with the melodies, and one day, instead of humming or la-la-ing, I began to sing.

Gary came bursting into the music room. Hearing my voice was as much a shock to him as it was to me. "That's nice!" he said. And then he picked up his horn, and added harmonies and fills to the melody.

As I sang, I began to cry: stretching my vocal chords was painful, but it also brought sadness for all the years I'd stifled my voice. Gary stayed with me: I would sing a verse, my throat would constrict, and then I'd sing some more, despite the sobs.

In November of 1975, he was offered a one-night engagement at Maidstone College of Art. It was the chance he'd been waiting for, to put together a band in his own name, and he quickly set about enlisting his favorite musicians—Rich Brunton, Laurie Allan and Bill MacCormick. He had even enticed Nick Mason, so there were two drummers. He not only wanted me to play but to perform two of my new compositions. I was singing, in my own fashion, every day now, and composing songs one after the other.

Even so, I was alarmed at the impressive line-up of musicians, and asked myself if I wasn't being too ambitious. But I was itching to play a gig, so I jumped in the deep end.

My other contribution was to find us free rehearsal space, in a rather rundown Georgian house at the bottom of Highgate West Hill that was owned by an eccentric divorcée who'd lived in the Hippie enclave of Tangiers, in Morocco. I had seen her first from our kitchen window, in her back garden, where she kept a horse and a donkey.

One day, I met her leading the basket-laden donkey down the hill, on her way to the shops. She was dressed in shorts and a straw hat, with only a scarf tied around her bosom. I stopped to say hello and stroke the donkey, and one thing led to another. She invited me to tea, and to play the Steinway grand in her drawing-room, a piano that David Bowie had played during a recent house party.

At rehearsal a few days later, while I was trying to control my nerves, the eyes of the tiger-skin that was draped across the piano seemed to be glaring at me. And then, as we counted off the first number, I felt a huge dark presence and turned to see the horse, being led past me, on a short-cut from the front door, through to the back garden.

The rehearsal was quite chaotic, and I could tell when it wound up that it would be the only one. I knew the others would pull it off on the night, but I had grave misgivings about how I would fare.

The journey to the concert was auspicious. Bill MacCormick remembered, and wrote: "Getting to Maidstone nearly proved to be the end of us all. Gary borrowed Nick's BMW to get us there. (Nick had a Pink Floyd meeting, and would come down later with a roadie.) In appalling weather, a large French lorry pulled out in front of us on the motorway and we passed it squeezed up against the central reservation, throwing gravel and grass everywhere. Had the car been anything other than a BMW, I suspect we would have bounced back under the lorry's wheels. It certainly got the adrenaline flowing!"

I remember the incident well, too: as Gary swerved to avoid the lorry, I glanced at him in panic, to gauge whether he was in control, and caught the steely expression in his eyes, more focused than I'd ever seen them. I think it was Laurie Allan who managed to say for all of us, "Good one, Gary!"

Nick arrived an hour or so later, looked at the car, made a pained expression, and shrugged. "By the way," he said. "How come my name's on the poster? I thought we'd asked them not to do that?" Nick had wanted to play a fun gig, away from Pink Floyd, and be like any other musician. He was clearly more concerned about his anonymity having been snafu-ed than about the large dent in his BMW.

"Ladies and gents, boys and girls, thank you for coming, hope you're having a good time," Gary shouted, and then counted, "One, two, three, four!" and we jumped straight into the first number, a blues instrumental.

I couldn't hear a note I was playing, despite the amps that had been set up by a Pink Floyd roadie. The only thing that reached my ears was a powerful wall of electric sound. When it came to my first song—"How Should I Know?—I couldn't tell if I was in or out of tune. Somehow, I went on through the numbers that included "Red River Valley," a sort of cowboy-folksong that was one of Gary's favorite standards; and managed to hold down the chords for "Aishalina," a composition based on a tune I'd learned in Tunisia, which I sang in Arabic, and over which Gary let rip with one of his searing solos. I was at least in the trend, as Eastern sounds were 'in,' compliments of The Beatles.

While I couldn't wait for the ordeal of my debut to be over, Gary was as happy as could be, as relaxed as ever as band leader, and made it seem that anyone could be up there doing what he was doing.

An hour or so later, when we came to the last number, he played his last high note, threw his right arm in the air, and pulled the band to a stop.

The set had gone down well; they were expert musicians

and knew how to entertain an audience. I, however, aghast at what I must have sounded like, was ready to give up playing. I left the stage, and skulked away from the others, to wallow in artistic angst. A young student who was walking by, came over. "That was great! I really liked your songs and your piano playing," he said, unaware that he'd offered the right words at just the right moment. My farewell to music was not to be. I'd taken my first wobbly steps and had been admitted to the men-only world of music.

Maidstone College of Art: l to r, Rich Brunton, Bill MacCormick; behind, Laurie Allan and Nick Mason.

The college invited Gary back for two additional recitals. He insisted I play with him on both occasions. The first concert was with three members of The Brotherhood of Breath—drummer Louis Moholo, bass-player Harry Miller, and trumpet player Harry Beckett—and was a blend of powerful rhythms and free improvisation. I can still recall being amazed that I was actually on stage with Louis at drums behind me, and can recall the intent

Backstage with Simon and Jamie, after the Maidstone duo gig.

Photo taken by Sharon Mumby

expression on his face as I turned to look at him.

The other concert, Gary and I played as a duo. We played together so often by then that we'd become symbiotic. One track from the first concert, and two from the duo, would be added to the same album as the jam sessions with Laurie Allan and Frank Perry, and released on the CD Avant Gardeners, thirty-two years later, in 2007. Clifford Allen, in *All About Jazz*, wrote: "The couple is sympathetic to the point of pronounced empathy...a really close duo engaged in constructive dialog...the effect is both incendiary and considered... Pam Windo's glassy pointillism slowly morphing into rolling churchy chords...that recalls Bobby Few...This release raises the profile of Pam Windo's playing considerably...and any further attention this might afford her is long overdue.

In a black and white photograph Gary must have taken after the duo performance, I am sitting with the boys, who had been in the audience. We are smiling, and close. We took the boys to all the gigs that weren't in rowdy bars or clubs, partly so they could enjoy the music, and partly because we rarely had extra money for a baby-sitter.

◆

At the end of that year, on December 14, Mongezi Feza died. He was just thirty. Quiet, smiling Mongs who played such forceful trumpet, and whom everybody loved, had gone.

Mongezi had been arrested for allegedly attacking a police officer who'd stopped him in the street for being disorderly. Mongezi was slim and just five feet tall, so it was hard to imagine him being much of a threat. We were in court when he stood in the witness box being arraigned, looking scared and confused; faced not with a welcoming audience but with the cold British judicial system. When the Judge asked how he pled, he looked all round like a frightened animal and then leaped over the box and made a run for it. Two officers grabbed hold of him and returned him to the box.

    His sentence was treatment at a psychiatric hospital where we visited him. Mongezi hadn't been himself for some while. To my mind, he'd never really adjusted from life in the South African townships, a looser, sunnier, if poorer life-style. In the cold congested northern capital, he had lost the will to live and to play. He died in hospital from double pneumonia which was diagnosed too late to save him. Harry Millers' wife Hazel raised funds to have his body sent back to South Africa, to honor his last words, "If anything happens to me, make sure I get back."

    We never knew if his arrest was a racial act. We never knew if the pneumonia was ignored. Gary was deeply saddened. "Yes, and I'm not going to live a long life either," I heard him say again, and turned away.

12

The new year of 1976 was hardly under way when I got a nice surprise. Nick Mason's wife Lindy called to ask if I'd like to go on holiday with her. England was at its bleakest, cold and dreary. She said she needed a break, somewhere in the sun.

Our two families had become quite close, in part because we were neighbors. Their super-modern house was in a secluded area at the top of Highgate West Hill. I loved going to visit them, to baby-sit, even to house-sit on occasion. We had a lot in common as well as music. We had young children: their two daughters were close enough in age to come for sleepovers with the boys. And we all loved good food, and swapped invitations for lunch or dinner. Nick often called to invite us to his favorite Indian restaurant in Hampstead. We were all partial to a good curry and when all the dishes were set on the table, between the eight of us, there was so much reaching and spooning, it turned into a frenzied food fest.

In return, we invited them to try our own home-made specialties, the sushi rolls and tempura and miso soup that I'd learned to make when a pair of Japanese girls stayed with us as lodgers. When guests came, we served meals on a low round table in the living-room. I recall asking Nick and Lindy if they minded sitting on the floor, Hippie-fashion. "Fine with me," Nick said, flopping onto the sisal carpet and crossing his legs.

Nick had become an archetype for me: the highly successful authoritative male figure. He was handsome and had an easy unassuming way about him. I felt attracted but never once thought of flirting with him because there was too much at stake. I didn't see it at the time, but I also censored myself because in his way, he took care of us.

When Nick was interviewed many years later in the Pink Floyd fan magazine, *Spare Bricks*, he said: "Gary was a really nice Guy and I liked Pam and the boys enormously as well. We both shared a similar sense of humor although Gary was without doubt a lot more volatile than me; perhaps with good reason. I had led a very sheltered existence in comparison. He was also an enormously accomplished player...any take was instantly usable... Gary probably respected my ability to achieve success with minimal talent, and believed I had organizational skills."

To be sure of sun, Lindy chose Antigua as our girls-only winter break. I decided the occasion warranted a new hairdo so I went to Brighton to see Gary's brother, Graham, who owned a hairdressing salon. I described a shaggy hairdo, something funkier than the straight short hair-style I had. The result was an abbreviated afro that did not flatter me at all. Lindy politely hid her shock but must have felt she was going on holiday with a different person than the one she'd invited.

After all our scrimping and saving, Antigua was a piece of paradise. The Pink Floyd office had booked us into a top-notch beach-front inn that stood amid lush green jungle on a hillside near English Harbor. We ate lobster and drank rum from coconuts, we spread our pale bodies with sun-tan lotion and lazed in the hot sun; we swam and sailed, and walked the seashore collecting shells. But it was only at night, in the dark, in our twin beds, with the therapeutic sound of waves lapping the shore that we talked about ourselves and our lives.

As well as being a dancer, Lindy was a classically-trained flautist. She'd recorded flute parts on *Green is the Colour*, Pink Floyd's soundtrack for the film *More*, and on "The Grand Vizier's Garden Party," on their *Ummagumma* album. Since then, as a wife and mother, she had quietly relinquished whatever musical ambitions she'd nurtured. She spoke about her husband's superstardom as if she were bearing witness: the huge stadium concerts, the weeks on end on the road and in the studio. I spoke of my own struggle to juggle playing and motherhood, but did not say that I was not about to give up.

Back home again, I recall it being chilly and the skies slate grey, and wishing we could all move somewhere in the sun.

And then one day that February, Gary came home to report we were going to visit John Paul Jones at the weekend, and "have a jam with him." John was the bass player with Led Zeppelin. I knew very little about the group, except that, at the time, it was the biggest rock band in the world. They'd recently released their new album *Presence*, and were moving away from complex arrangements and ballads to guitar-based jams, which, I thought, partly explained the idea of a jam with us.

Gary wasn't going because of John's fame. He was unimpressed by fame and remained himself in the company of stars. It was a quality that I passed on to the boys. I would never tell them which of our friends and acquaintances was or wasn't famous. That way they would approach people on their own terms.

We drove down to John's mansion in Sussex. Taking over the country estates of impoverished aristocrats was one of the rewards of rock stardom: rock music trumped class.

John came out of the house to greet us, accompanied by a sleek ivory-haired dog that must have been a Borzoi. Apart from his long curly hair, he looked like an ordinary guy, dressed in blue jeans and shirt. I was discovering that off-stage, rock stars looked like the rest of us. On-stage was another matter: they either resembled, 'Jesus in crushed-velvet flares,' or strutted around in tight satin pants and low-cut spandex tops, which made me wonder if they weren't trying to upstage women, just as we were liberating ourselves from such provocative garments.

John took us on a tour of his house which was done out in rich veneered oak paneling. He introduced us to his wife and led us upstairs to the nursery where his three young daughters were playing with their nanny. The boys' eyes widened at the array of toys, and so we left them to play.

It was late when we moved into the music room and John rolled a joint. I took a toke and recall sitting at the shiny black Steinway, looking around at the array of guitars, banjos, violins, cellos, and collection of African and Indian instruments, and wondering how many John Paul could play.

The marijuana slowed us down. The two men rapped about music while they set up their instruments. I was feeling mildly stoned and wondering what would come out of me—with free improvisation, it was as much a surprise to the player as it was to the audience.

I recall being the one to start, setting down some chords in a basic rhythm. I felt the fingered notes of John's upright bass reverberate through me. Gary waited for his cue, for the feel to settle, and then slid into the groove, at first a few notes, tentatively, and then he built to a hard and insistent solo. After some time like that, we moved into the free zone, away from recognizable chords and rhythm patterns to notes and sounds that we each created in the moment, to answer or provoke. And then, in unison, we morphed back to the original chords and groove.

That night, I shared in a flight of fancy, or rather, two skilled musicians allowed me to add my still-inexpert but fervent dance on piano. We didn't play tunes, we didn't play blues: we just explored the spectrum of sounds that could come from our instruments. Fred Frith once described how he'd started his band

Henry Cow with fellow musician Tim Hodgkinson: "He had an alto sax, and I had my violin, and we just improvised this ghastly screaming noise for about half an hour."

Gary had not brought the reel-to-reel, seeing it as an intrusion in someone's house, famous or not. I wish he had; I would give anything to hear it now. I never saw John again. That was how it often went; you came together for a moment's creative blast and then went your separate ways.

◆

It was about now that my flings were interrupted. The word fling—*"a short period of enjoyment or wild behavior"* notes the Oxford Dictionary—makes it all sound too flippant. Even fun doesn't describe what I was doing. Looking back, as objectively as I can, it seems an enigma: I didn't have sex just to have sex; nor was I looking for a man to love, because I had one. It was an affirmation of life, of energy, the sharing of sexual pleasure, like sharing music and good food. To encompass a new man into my life, even briefly—a man with whom there was mutual attraction—was more erotic than sexual. Way before us, in 1939, Denis de Rougemont wrote in *Love in the Western World*: "Sexuality is the instinct which directs the individual to the objectives of the species. Eroticism is sexual pleasure for its own sake. Amorous passion is infinite desire." He also wrote: "A more convivial vision of community may be emerging, one with a new ethic of love, having as a goal the full and authentic freedom of a real person: *the control, not of others, but of oneself."* After the strict and hypocritical mores of the Victorian era, and of postwar conservatism, we had taken up the Hippies' gauntlet, forerunners in experimenting with this concept.

The man I fell in erotic love with was tall and lanky with floppy fair hair, and was a master carpenter. I must have had a soft spot for carpenters. Bob Dylan made it make sense for me:"His clothes are dirty but his hands are clean...Lay, lady, lay. Lay across my big brass bed." I pursued the man relentlessly until, despite him having a steady girlfriend, he gave in and bundled me into his drafty Army Jeep. There were no romantic games on my part: he knew I would return to my husband. But he was more than interested in the sex, bemused and curious all at once. I enjoyed being with him, and showing him about myself and my body. I was acting out the exchange of roles: until then, women believed men knew all about sex, that women were by nature passive. And here I was, showing a man what eroticism was all about.

Our affair lasted a few months, and I wasn't particularly discreet. It was a fine line, I sensed—but did not always see—between the attraction that made me want sex with a man, and the attraction that made me fall in love. The only thing I knew was that it was all in the eyes. Rumi said: "Lovers don't finally meet somewhere. They're in each other all along."

◆

Meanwhile, Gary was becoming increasingly successful, which meant a bit more money in the family coffers. There were still the frequent foreign tours, to Germany, The Netherlands, and France.

At home, musicians continued to come to our flat to hang out. There'd be new albums to play and discuss; dancing, joking, excitement about all the projects and possibilities that we saw going on around us. We got high on music and camaraderie. "And those who were seen dancing were thought to be insane by those who could not hear the music," wrote Nietzsche.

Family life flowed through it all, with its own rhythm, a rhythm that was of course flexible. On Saturdays, we shopped at Camden farmers' market, filling our modest fridge to the brim with fresh vegetables, fish and meat. On Sundays, we would take the boys on paper chases or for picnics on Hampstead Heath. He would take his flute to practice among the willows and beech trees.

He loved to go walking too, and took the boys with him all over London. One day they made it all the way back from Greenwich where they'd been to see the Cutty Sark—a walk of some seven miles through central London.

Every other weekend the boys went to Brighton. By now, we saw them off at Victoria Station and they traveled the hour-long journey alone on the train. It was the only time that he and I were just a couple. We liked nothing better than to go riding side by side on the two second-hand bicycles he had fixed up for us. London was quiet on Sundays, around sleepy Hampstead village, even along the tree-lined streets of Notting Hill and Holland Park.

The boys played outside all day long. It was part of our philosophy that they should be as free as we had been when we were children, exploring without our supervision. I did not feel they 'belonged' to me, or that I had to mold them in any way. Because of this, it took us a while to discover the survivors' camp they had constructed in the spinney of our grounds. It was made from old doors and rugs and broken-down chairs they'd rummaged for in our building's dark and dirty basement. The camp had become their second home; a place to go, they explained, when nuclear war broke out and the world ended.

On cold or rainy days, they'd hunker down in their bedroom, where the bunk beds became a fort with hundreds of soldiers, some of them toys, others drawn on the sheets. Often, they'd find their way into the music room. Rather than have them taught, we let them explore sounds, as I myself was doing, and we'd hear them singing the songs they composed, squawking notes on the trumpet, or beating the drums that Robert had left behind, a set that had once belonged to Keith Moon, The Who's notorious drummer.

We overheard them once, arguing: "No, don't play it in four time! Play it in three!" They'd got 'three-time' and playing 'free' mixed up. As well as excelling at play, they were doing well at school too, though we didn't nag them about homework or grades.

He was not a businessman in any sense of the word, and never earned enough from music to stop taking other jobs. But he was careful with money without being penny pinching, and knew what we could and could not spend. It was a pragmatic sleight of hand, not given to many artists. The extra jobs he took on were as varied as his musical tastes. He didn't buy into the starving artist ideal. Even so, he would have done almost anything rather than put on a suit and tie and work in an office. "Getting on the stage and just playing...isn't enough, you've got to live a way of life...the washing-up or cleaning or making sure someone's there to look after the kids or that the car's fixed or that we go to the shopping mall," he would say quite vehemently to other musicians, when the occasion arose.

Most of the odd jobs he did were physically challenging. But he was strong and had the stamina of an athlete, and I never once heard him complain that the jobs took away from his music. When our budget needed an extra boost, he worked for a moving company, packing boxes, lifting furniture and driving a delivery truck around London. I remember him, dressed for work in cargo pants and a grey tank top, and shiny with sweat. He would pop home if he'd made a local delivery, to grab a sandwich and a cup of tea. He'd sit in the kitchen and have a quick read of *The Sun*, including an ogle of Page Three's busty pin-up picture which I always checked out over his shoulder: lacking such endowments, it was a daily provocation for me. "Even when I was driving a truck for quite a long time, I wasn't happy about the situation but I was happy about my playing," he commented, when asked.

The rent for the beautiful flat that had at first seemed such a rash choice, miraculously, went down, not up. A diligent resident discovered the building's owners had illegally increased the rent some years before, which forced them to go back to the original rent before making an increase. In all the time we lived there, we never defaulted; nor did we borrow from either a bank or family. Had we bought the flat back then, we'd have eventually become millionaires.

Perhaps my favorite photograph of that time is of us mugging for the camera, in the midst of painting the hall, rollers in hand, a tray of white paint at our feet. We're wearing paint caps, spattered jeans and T-shirts, and look happy and carefree. The photograph speaks of an era, of a generation, of a time for us that was fun loving, uncomplicated, and unpretentious in its outlook.

Taking a break from painting our big white flat.

He had a passion, too, for cars of all types and watched with great nostalgia the Sixties' American models that featured in movies. One day, he came home beaming. Nick Mason had hired him to help out in the garage where he restored his collection of vintage Maseratis. "He was general gofer and was great company...useful for the other end of the spanner! But he did suffer a bit at the hands of the regular mechanics," Nick would joke years later, in a magazine interview.

The two men couldn't have been more different: Nick from upper-class stock, a trained architect; Gary, from the middle class, a cook and merchant seaman. Nick was from the highly-produced Pink Floyd-school of rock, Gary from the school of soulful jazz improvisation. The glue that held them together was music and a shared sense of humor. Nick would say later that it was Gary's "insane ebullience" that attracted people. They shared too a fanatical love of cars. Nick would come to our flat to play miniature car racing with Gary and the boys, on the Scalectrix track we left assembled in our long hallway. Then, they were just four boys sprawled about, playing with cars made to scale, a collection that Nick would often bring his own models to add to.

The garage job satisfied Gary's love of tinkering with all things mechanical, large or small. When it wasn't cars, he would sit in the kitchen for hours polishing his saxophone with a rag, removing all the keys one by one to clean off the stains of accumulated spittle. He knew his instrument down to the last key-pad and rarely took it to be fixed.

One day, while working in the back driveway on the little Citroën 2CV van that had replaced our VW Camper, a neighbor took it in his head to offer him one of his two Volvo P1800s. "Man! He's giving it to us on permanent loan!" Gary said, slapping my hand in a celebratory hi-five when he came up to report on this windfall. With this car—a red version of the white one actor Roger Moore drove in *The Saint*—we moved up in the world.

By then, we had swapped our Hippie attire for more contemporary clothes, including leather jackets, and jeans without patches. My perm had at last grown out and my hair was now cut in a bob and shining with henna. His hair was cut neatly too, his Hippie mustache and sideburns gone. Over the years, he would experiment with whatever style he felt like, from clean-cut, to shaggy, or spiky. Sometimes he went beardless; at other times he sported a well-manicured beard, which, with his steel-rimmed glasses, gave him a serious look, like one of the more intellectual jazz men on the scene.

✦

The bouts of asthma were coming more often. I looked into cures; he tried acupuncture but it was a stubborn illness, and he had to rely on the inhaler to manage the breathlessness. Sometimes, when he had an attack in the night, I would massage his back, to help him relax and breathe. Once, it was so bad I had to take him to Highgate Hospital for steroid treatments.

I continued composing and jamming, and was fired with enthusiasm about the few gigs I'd done and impatient for more. As for jobs, I'd gone from barmaid, to the roadie gigs, to packing moving boxes, and to a short-lived stint as auxiliary nurse in a maternity ward. My younger son had been born at home with the help of a midwife and the new breathing techniques, an experience that had deeply affected me. In my crisp nurse's uniform I felt blessed to help take care of all the new-born babies. But it was a calling I soon saw would take a lot of time and dedication, so I abandoned it.

In a local newspaper, I finally found a better-paid and more convenient job as part-time secretary at William Ellis School for Boys, just a hundred yards down the road from Brookfield Mansions.

13

Sometime in April of 1976, when Gary was chomping at the bit to record his own music, Nick Mason offered him free time in Britannia Row, Pink Floyd's brand-new state-of-the-art studio. Gary would be the first in, and would test its systems and quality. From the moment he heard this, he went into top gear. He knew exactly what music he wanted to record, and which musicians he wanted to use. The sessions became known as the Steam Radio Tapes. Gary just came up with the name; his titles were always 'off-the-wall.' I think this one came to mind because he saw himself as an old-fashioned player dealing with ultra-modern recording techniques. In keeping, he kept a handwritten log on sheets of drawing paper, of the tracks, the musicians and the dates.

The first track we recorded was one of my compositions, its title, coincidentally, "Is this the Time?" I'd composed the piece as an exercise after a lesson with jazz pianist Peter Lemer, who was playing with Ginger Baker and his Baker Gurvitz Army at the time.

We were all gathered in the glassed-in studio, headphones and microphones at the ready. It was my first time in a studio and though I felt nervous, it helped that I had played with most of the musicians before. Nick sat across from me behind his Premier drum kit. Hugh Hopper was one of the two bass players Gary had called in. He was a lanky man with a droopy mustache who always wore a knitted skull cap, and had a droll sense of humor. By then, we'd become fast friends and had spent many family weekends with Hugh and his girlfriend on his torpedo-boat home on the Thames Estuary.

The second bass-player was Bill MacCormick, who I knew from the Maidstone gig. Bill was 'Mr. Cool,' old-school in a corduroy jacket, but with long fly-away hair. Rich Brunton was on guitar. I had a soft spot for Rich; with his slim build and toothsome smile, he had the look of a boy about him. We'd been through a lot together too, from the terrible Swiss trip to the Maidstone gig. I remember he once said of us: "I love watching you two. You're like a traveling circus!"

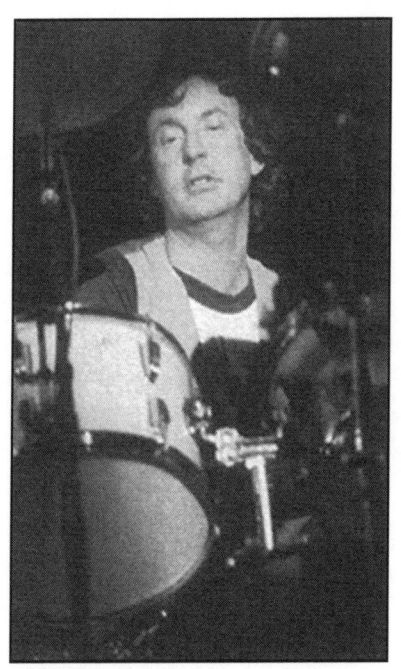

Nick Mason on drums.

Brian Humphries, Pink Floyd's chief engineer, sat at the console in the glass booth, taking the change of music and pace in his stride. I hadn't written charts, so I played the head riff several times until one by one the musicians jumped in and followed the pattern from the top. On the third take, we played on through to a long groove that would have solos and vocals added to it later. They were such accomplished musicians they had taken my simple riff and rhythm and made my composition sound accomplished too.

Robert would come into the studio a week or so later, to

add the lyrics I'd written: "Is this the time? Now is the Time. The present is now. Give me the present of your time." And I sang the back-up vocal, repeating over and over, *Is this the time?*

Some time in May, we were back in Britannia Row, ready to record "Letting Go," the second of my compositions. "...Two hearts entwined, two souls that know...bodies that learn the warmth of touch, hands that glow, and eyes that know, the feel of love and letting go." I didn't tell Gary who my songs were about, and he never asked. Most of the time, I didn't know myself. But this one was clearly about us. Improvising was about freedom from rules; my songs were about love. To give the song its best shot, I asked Julie Tippetts if she would sing it.

Of all the memories I have of those sessions, this one stands out most. The musicians who'd played on the track were gathered around the console listening as Julie stood in front of the microphone and clasped the headphones to her ears. Her voice was so beautiful and clear it blew us away. There was for me, though, an inexpressible sadness that I could not sing my own song as beautifully as she was singing it. We all held our breath as Julie came to the end of her second take with a soaring high note that she held onto for what seemed like minutes before ending the song with a sigh—a perfect ending for 'letting go.'

On through that year, whenever there was a time slot, we hurried off to Brit Row, as it was now called. By mid-summer, in June, we enjoyed that rarest of things in England, a heat wave. Day after day for two weeks, we saw only blue skies and ninety degree temperatures. Everyone came out of their chilly reserve, wore sun-dresses and short-sleeved shirts, had fun and got suntans, and it was easy to see that if every summer were like that, my country's culture would quickly become more open and relaxed.

Gary felt at home in the studio, working closely with Nick, who both produced and played drums. Nick enjoyed time out from his own group's highly-sophisticated recording sessions.

Gary and me, listening to takes in Britannia Row.

"When Pink Floyd records, we're slaves to perfection," he said, with a hint of regret in his voice.

Without lengthy deliberation, Gary now put down several of his own compositions—"Ginkie," a sweet bass clarinet solo dedicated to his grandfather; "Healing Line" (which he later renamed "Sweetest Angel"); "Stand Fast" (a re-recording of a track originally played by Symbiosis), as well as his favorite standard, "Red River Valley."

For these tracks, which were more complex than mine, he brought in two keyboardists. One was Mike Hugg who'd co-founded the Manfred Mann Band, and who was a jazz man at heart. Mike and his wife lived in a little mews house in Hampstead where we'd often visit them for dinner, and spend the evening talking about music. The other keyboard player was Gary Moberley, an Aussie who happened to be a neighbor in Brookfield Mansions. He had just finished playing with Elton John on his "Louder than Concorde" tour, and would go on to play and tour with The Sweet, The Bee Gees and Little Richard. Bill MacCormick and Hugh Hopper continued to cover the bass parts, and Peter van Hooke came in to take over drumming when Nick was producing.

◆

In February of 1977, Queen Elizabeth II and the whole country celebrated Her Majesty's Silver Jubilee, twenty-five dutiful years on England's throne. It was also the year the World Trade Center was completed in New York, the year Amnesty International won the Nobel Peace Prize, and the Egyptian President Anwar Sadat recognized Israel.

We, meanwhile, continued with our sessions whenever Nick called to say Brit Row was available. The studio had become our second home. The boys often came with us and watched the goings-on from couches in the control room. We'd see the roadies coming in and out, Pink Floyd's manager, Steve O'Rourke, buzzing around in the office, and Roger Waters poring over lyrics. I was standing next to him one day when he was going through "Sheep" from *Animals*. "…When cometh the day we lowly ones, through quiet reflection, and great dedication, master the art of karate, Lo, we shall rise up, and then we'll make the bugger's eyes water."

We recorded the last of Gary's compositions, a track called, "Missy," and my third composition, "Come into my Garden," a rippling sort of jazz theme on which Terri Quaye sang the lyrics and played congas. Terri, whose father was Cab Quaye, a well-known entertainer of Ghanaian descent, gave music workshops and had taken me under her wing for a while to help build my technique and confidence.

The understanding with Nick was that when we had recorded enough tracks, he would try to sell the album. It had not dawned on Gary that it might help to keep the music to a recognizable category. Despite Nick's best efforts, the album would prove too eclectic to find a home. "I've tried," he reported, reluctantly. "It's a difficult time to sell this kind of music." He also remarked that, "no-one in the band looked like Marc Bolan." It would have been just after this that glam-rocker Bolan, who sold more records than Jimi Hendrix and The Who, died in a car accident, at age twenty-nine. We were up against the new rage for glam-rock, disco music, not to mention the Punk movement that had by now taken a serious hold on the musical arena.

About the album, Nick later said: "I think we all thought it would be good to try and make a more polished record than the usual jazz jam session feel that a lot of jazz based-records used to have. There was little point in using me and a state of the art studio to make a live or home sounding recording. It would be nice to think I did make it sound a little more polished..."

In 1994, Robert would add "Is this the Time?"—using the refrain *Now is the Time?* as the title—to his album *Flotsam Jetsam*. But it would be twenty years after the Britannia Row recordings when Michael King insisted that Gary rummage through the boxes in his garage to unearth the tapes so that he could re-master three of the tracks for what would prove to be the posthumous album, *His Master's Bones;* a title Gary would come up with before his passing.

Eventually, to my great surprise, while I was writing this memoir, the album was finally released in its entirety by Gonzo, in the U.K.
I smiled when one of the reviewers wrote that "Come into My Garden" reminded him of King Crimson.

◆

Although we'd heard Punk brewing since the early Seventies, it had made its first dramatic appearance the year before, when The Damned released their single, "New Rose." Nick Mason would be asked to produce the group's follow-up album, *Music for Pleasure*. I recall Nick joking with us about how he should address band member Rat Scabies: "Should I say hello Rat, or hello Mr. Scabies?"

With the recession, the working class was bearing the brunt, and the rock-star rebellion that had been the first to challenge the status-quo by earning fantastic amounts of money playing loud music, and having fun doing it, was now being challenged by the riveting anger of the Punks.

My husband took to Punk as he took to everything that was strikingly authentic, applauding. I can still hear him, as he swept the floor in his underpants, imitating Ian Dury's thick Cockney accent as he sang along, "Sex and drugs and rock 'n' roll is all my brain and body need." Behind the scenes, Dury had had to apologize to jazzman Ornette Coleman for ripping off a riff played by his bass-player Charlie Haden; which was followed by Coleman's own apology for having ripped it off an old English tune.

The Punks' stance, clothes and lyrics were so powerfully rough and ready, they couldn't fail to be seen and heard. They weren't into art and poetry, or even music, but were voicing their anger at poverty, inequality and unemployment. Even while we understood their message, we agreed with the general feeling that with the Punks, the optimism of the Sixties and Seventies and the poetic lyrics and melodies of rock and pop, were 'disappearing down the drain.'

Although I played avant-garde music, at first I considered the Punks too extreme. Their credo, *"Anyone can do it,"* went against what I had believed for so long, (but wasn't exactly living out). When the Sex Pistols had seen fit to bring out their "God Save the Queen" single in May of that Jubilee year, I had cringed on hearing the lyrics: "...They made you a moron... God save the Queen... She ain't no human being."

Eventually, I would come to see that Punk took our free improvisation philosophy to its natural conclusion, especially when Johnny Rotten, the lead vocalist with The Sex Pistols replied to press criticism: "You gotta learn to sing," with: "Why?

Who writes the rules?"

It was with the Punk movement that I saw the emergence of more women into the music world's spotlight. The names and bands I most remember were the raucous The Slits, and Siouxsie and the Banshees, with its mix of Punk, pop, and avant-garde. In America, the girl band Joan Jett and The Runaways was so big that Cheap Trick and Tom Petty both opened for them. I found myself envying these women, their sexual bravado in lyrics, costumes, and stage shows, and had no idea that it wouldn't be long before I was doing something similar myself.

But, that year, for me, nothing could compete with Fleetwood Mac's exquisite album, *Rumours*. I was in awe of all the tracks, but especially "Dreams." "You say you want your freedom. Well who am I to keep you down. Players only love you when they're playing. Say...women...they will come and they will go...When the rain washes you clean...you'll know." The album became part of my daily life; I played it over and over. The album was a timeless classic. While re-reading this part about Fleetwood Mac, some thirty-six years after its release, "Go Your Own Way" was playing on the local radio station.

And then, in the fall, Joan Armatrading came out with *Love and Affection*, an album that knocked everyone off their feet. Her rich voice and daring honesty got her quickly up in the charts and inspired me both musically and emotionally, especially the title song, with its simple sentiment: "I am not in love but open to persuasion. Just make love, with affection." Gary had played on a session with Joan some time before the album came out, and had come home afterwards saying what a great lady she was.

Sometime early that summer, perhaps inspired by the sun, I came up with the idea of a women's group. After a long season surrounded by men, I turned to women to give balance to my life. The women friends I'd made were of the same persuasion; and the word sisterhood was in the air. I wanted to make up for what I saw as lost time, for all the years I'd been in men's thrall, and had put off being close to other women. The old culture that had focused only on our being marriageable had made rivals, if not enemies, of us all.

Five of us in our late twenties and thirties took turns to host a session in which we shared our creative skills. One friend was an artist and got us to make a collage to express how we saw ourselves. We were from different backgrounds, had different hopes and ambitions but we were all going through similar experiences and emotions about our lives and our men. We didn't bitch about men but focused on ourselves: this, I felt, was a winning formula.

A French friend gave us a lesson in French cooking, and I got to practice my long-lost French with her too. She reminded me of the French singers I'd listened to, so I bought the sheet music for "Je ne Regrette Rien," and "La Vie en Rose," and tried my own renditions of Edith Piaf's songs. I did the same with Marlene Dietrich's "Falling in Love Again," imagining myself in a smoke-filled bar, and talk-singing: "Men flit around me, like moths to the flame, and if they burn, I can't help it."

I gave my women's group session in the hallway of our flat, demonstrating basic karate kicks and punches. I explained that it wasn't about being able to beat a man up if we were threatened—which for most women wasn't an option—but to have a couple of techniques ready to get out of a bad situation, and to not think of oneself as a victim in the first place.

From what I read, the women's groups in America were much more radical—everything was more radical in America—and focused on equal legal and social rights. Their advocates insisted that all women wanted more than their lives offered. I certainly wanted more—to be something beyond a wife, mother and sexual partner—something that fulfilled me as a person. I often wondered if my mother and my sister, and my old friends wanted more of anything; but decided that they would have been doing something about it if they did.

My friend Lindy came to one session, but her free time

was mostly taken up with a group of women potters. I went with her one evening to Judy Waters' house. Judy had recently gotten divorced from Roger Waters, Pink Floyd's bass player. She looked anything but depressed, a vivacious blonde, clearly from the upper-middle class. The English have lived so long with class consciousness it comes naturally to know who's who. But Judy also lived in a world where you put on a good show and a good face, come what may.

I spent several evenings in this 'circle of energy,' quietly working with clay in Judy's garden studio. She seemed to be in a phallic phase, producing a series of tall filigree cylinders with domed tops; perhaps working through the tumult of her husband's superstardom and the sexiness of the rock star world. I made a small vase, and a sea-green sake pot that I still have. And both Lindy and Judy went on to become successful master potters.

As a result of spending more time with women, one day when Gary was away playing, I maneuvered a three-some with my artist friend and her boyfriend. Free love activities did not just happen by themselves, at least not in my experience. Someone had to take the initiative. When I invited them over, the friend knew without saying. I brought out some wine, put on some smooth music and the love-in happened. We lay in the dark, barely aware of facial expressions, just three naked bodies. Revealing one's body to others—man or woman—was one of the aims of free love: the removal of shame.

As a child, I had longed for physical contact. My mother had not been given to touching and displays of affection; her strict guardian Aunt had seen to that. My sister seemed to have taken after her, which left me with the sole affection of my father.

Now, it was that triangle, my friend, her man, and me, enjoying the pleasures and revelations of mixed nudity and of shared touching. But at the point when the man did to me what men do, everything fell apart. In that moment of pain that she had not expected, the friend denounced me: "I told you she was a sexy cow!"

We continued to be friends and though talking and working through dramas was what women were doing, whatever we had learned or not learned that night remained unsaid.

◆

Gary's music card continued to fill up, and included people like *wunderkind* guitarist Chris Spedding, who'd played on The Vibrators single, "Pogo Dancing." He was called for a recording session with American punk-rocker Suzie Quatro, who was more popular in England than in the U.S. and had just had a hit with her single, "Can the Can." "...Try to can the can...," (which meant, try to get your man to commit).

I clearly recall sitting in our living room with Foreigner's drummer Dennis Elliott who had come over to talk to Gary about forming a band of his own. It seemed all musicians imagined a band of their own. Dennis was still with Foreigner a few years later, in 1981, for their big hit "Urgent," when, to Gary's undying disappointment, it was American sax giant Junior Walker—one of his all-time heroes—who played the riveting solo on the track.

Much the same thing happened with Joe Jackson who was relatively unknown before his first hit, "Is She Really Going out with Him?" Joe's influences were as varied as Gary's, and included Soft Machine. Like Elvis Costello, Joe challenged the Punks and eventually created his own 'new wave' style.

Another unlikely candidate Gary got hooked up with was Donovan. He didn't bring Donovan home but was involved with him for a while. It was a decade or so after his blockbuster hits, "Mellow Yellow," "Sunshine Superman," and "Jennifer Juniper." Donovan's gentle blend of folk, jazz and psychedelic pop had symbolized England's own 'flower power' years, but that era was over and already being ridiculed for its naïveté. When the harsher message of Punk moved in, artists like Donovan were moved out;

he'd even gone to live in the countryside, as if in exile. I clearly remember Gary coming back from meeting him and telling me: "He doesn't know where to go next." But Donovan wasn't the only one experiencing this dilemma and it wasn't something Gary could fix.

This wasn't the case for Paul Rodgers, the sexy lead singer who'd gone from success with the band Free to success with his own band, Bad Company. I first met Paul at a karate tournament in which Gary and I were taking part. Paul practiced the same style as we did, and was as mad about karate as Gary—perhaps even more so. He had even worked up a kata demonstration—a complex series of karate moves, like a dance—that he performed to a track of his band's music.

As I watched him that day, it was easy to see that he was the ultimate performance artist.

I recall the evening Paul invited us to dinner in his chic townhouse. We were greeted by his beautiful Japanese wife, who was holding on her lap a baby and a very young child, both of whom looked exactly like her, not at all like Paul, and I couldn't help wondering how he felt about that.

Paul was kind enough to give me the keys to his country house so that I could go into hiding for a week and do what jazz musicians call 'wood-shedding.' I worked and sang, but it was strange to be completely alone, after the boisterous company of my husband and children.

✦

One morning that autumn, I heard the phone ring, followed by a yell that warranted my running into the hall to find out what had happened.

"Remember the buddy from the Merchant Navy?" Gary asked. "He's in London!" He was thrilled because he and Ian had lost touch since his deportation.

Ian was over at our flat within the hour. He was a tall lean man, with short ash-blond hair and pale blue eyes; reticent and laid-back. There were hugs and jokes and then, "I knew you'd make a name for yourself one day, Gaz," he said. He told us how he'd kept an eye out for Gary's name in the music magazines and had finally seen it—Robert's Drury Lane concert. He'd contacted Virgin Records who provided our phone number. He'd been planning to come to England to see his elderly mother in Brighton; finding Gary was the impetus he needed.

Ian stayed a week, catching up, talking a good deal about music, getting tips from Gary for his saxophone playing. When he left, we took his address. That we would all meet again in America never entered our heads.

14

It was in that summer of 1977, a sunny and breezy day in August. The dark waves of the English Channel were splashing against the side of the ferry. We were on deck, bound for Calais—me, Gary, and the boys, and the members of The Carla Bley Band. Carla Bley was an American avant-garde jazz pianist whose big band was becoming very popular, both in America and Europe.

Carla had chosen Gary like an art connoisseur, with an experienced eye for what fitted her taste. She was tall and thin, with an electrified mop of ash-blonde hair. Gary raved about her idiosyncratic style of music and how clever her arrangements were. It was a mixed pill to swallow: I was in aching awe of her unique talent and charisma but was pleased too that he'd found a kindred spirit instead of another Doris Troy or Norma Green. Carla was the epitome of a female jazz pianist. Luckily, I felt no jealousy, as I sensed it was a strong musical kinship that had attracted them to each other. "They joke, they bicker, they frolic... and it's this intensive closeness that gives The Carla Bley Band its fresh onstage 'looseness' as well as its astounding musical tightness," was reported by one reviewer.

I also knew that Carla and I would never be friends; she had long ago broken the male barrier and was in her own men-only club—I never saw her in the company of another woman, except for her daughter.

The European tour was to include the *Jazz à Juan* festival in Antibes, where we were headed first. The boys and I were allowed to go along with Gary because I'd booked a gig for Carla for the one night she was in London to pick up the British band members—Gary, Hugh Hopper and Elton Dean. Dingwall's Club in Camden Lock was owned by a friend and I managed to convince him that Carla's zany brand of avant-garde jazz would go down well there. The gig was a stunning success: the queue for each of the two performances stretched right down the street.

I'd also arranged for our old friend, the nude photographer from Brighton, to be the tour's driver-cum-roadie, and to find us a decent bus. He'd had plenty of experience driving Land Rovers in Europe and North Africa.

When the ferry docked in Calais, we drove on to Paris, where smart hotel rooms had been booked for us, as well as a slap-up dinner. We were so late arriving that the waiters were standing in the dark street, white napkins on their arms, looking out for us.

The next morning, we continued the long drive south during which I had time to meet the American contingent: trombonist Roswell Rudd and drummer Andrew Cyrille were both highly-respected veterans of the American jazz scene. Along with Carla's husband, Michael Mantler, on trumpet, there was Bob Stewart on tuba and John Clarke on French horn. Because Carla mostly conducted her band, only playing piano on certain numbers, she had brought along pianist Terry Adams for the others. With his Thelonious Monk-Jerry Lee Lewis style, Terry perfectly suited her compositions. When we stopped at a roadside bistro for lunch, while all the others were keen to try French cuisine—*steak frites* being the most popular—Terry, who was from Kentucky, would only eat the peanut butter and Ritz crackers he'd brought with him for such emergencies.

Just a few days before we'd left England, on August 16,

Elvis Presley had died from a heart attack, and from an arsenal of drugs. He was forty-two. The King was dead: the King in white satin who'd become a parody, but still a brilliant one, of the phenomenal young rock 'n' roller whose voice and sexuality had lit up the world. There were few who did not shed a tear, knowing how much he had suffered. He'd become famous just at the moment a teenager is setting out to find himself, and had been led by people who did not care for anything except his money and celebrity.

Gary and Terry Adams commiserated. "I first met Gary in 1977, in London, for the beginning of The Carla Bley Band's European tour. The first thing we talked about was what a weird world it was going to be without Elvis Presley. The next day he showed me a street full of mourning Elvis guys in leather jackets," Terry would write, some fifteen years later, after Gary too had passed away.

Antibes was a-buzz with music and crowds of jazz fans. Carla's band gave two performances. During the first one, she enlisted the boys to play tambourines on a couple of numbers, as a gimmick. By then, the boys thought nothing of being on stage before a large audience, and grinned and bopped around in their multi-colored striped T-shirts, having a great time.

The Carla Bley Band, Italy, 1977. Gary is trying to use his flip-flops as headphones.

When the band was packed and ready to drive on to their next performance in Munich, Gary accompanied me and the boys to the train station. We were going on to visit friends from London who now lived in the mountains near Perpignan. The train ride was a treat, and ran alongside the sparkling Mediterranean. My friend Lilli met us and drove us up to Mas Domingo, a stone farmhouse with dramatic views of the French Pyrenees.

Lilli was German, her husband George, a South African, and an old friend of Chris McGregor's. Lilli had just recently given birth to a baby girl, and George was holding her in his arms outside the farmhouse to greet us. Lilli's nephew was there too, a new friend for the boys to play with.

The weather was glorious, the scenery stunning and life in the farmhouse relaxing. One day, we hiked into the mountains, all the way to Ceret, the village where Picasso, Matisse and Braque had all lived at different times. Sometimes we drove down to a deserted beach on the coast, to cool down with hours of swimming. My elder son had to paddle around with a heavily-bandaged left arm held up in the air. A week before we'd left, he'd thrust it through a pane of glass during a game of hide-and-seek, and the stitches were too recent to get wet.

Before we left to go home, we helped out for a whole day with the harvest of potatoes and a small crop of cannabis. To celebrate this bounty, a home-grown pig was roasted and we sat in the field under the stars all night, eating and drinking, and smoking joints.

◆

The day the blue airmail letter from America fell onto our doormat is etched clearly into my memory. It was from Carla Bley. I had known it would come but hadn't wanted to think about it. The letter—transatlantic telephoning still cost too much—was an invitation for Gary to join her band for a tour in the U.S. the following January. Gary was jubilant and jumped up and down, shouting, "Yeah! Yeah!"

And then the reality hit him: deportation was non-negotiable. He wasn't one to sulk so when he fell into despondency, thinking it impossible, my coming-to-the-rescue instinct got stirred up. I would go to New York to see if I could somehow acquire a visa for him. As usual, I jumped in head first, without any idea how I would do this.

I arrived in the first week of November and found the Big Apple in the midst of an Indian summer. The sun and warmth certainly improved my first impression of a city I'd had no desire to see. I walked along the avenues, wandered around Soho, and the East and West Village, fascinated but feeling sad that the first time I saw the city Gary loved so much, it was without him.

I stayed at Carla's New York office. One day, I picked up the phone and dialed the number for the Musicians' Union. By a stroke of good luck, or perhaps because his secretary was at lunch, I got hold of someone quite high up. I explained our need for a visa, and the voice responded: "Come on over to my office, hon. Let's see if I can help you sort things out."

I sat across the desk from a friendly rotund gentleman who told me "very confidentially," "You must fill out Question [-] of the visa application: *Gary Windo is the only musician who can play the Highgate Stomp.*" He knew very well there was no such tune. "That should do the trick," he said, shaking my hand.

Before I went home to report this good news to Gary, I met music producer Hal Willner for the first time. He was a devoted fan of avant-garde music, especially of Carla's band, and had already become a fan of Gary's. Over lunch, I listened to Mr. Willner's stories about all the new music he was either already producing or wanted to produce. In a couple of years, he would become music coordinator for Saturday Night Live; and, to my great surprise, would use one of my songs—"Great Expectations"—as a juke-box number in an SNL sketch.

Back in London, Gary and I marched up the steps of the American Consulate and just as the friendly man in New York had vouchsafed, Gary was given a fully-stamped H2 visa for an eighteen-month trip to the U.S., on the basis that he was the only musician who could play, "The Highgate Stomp." Gary looked at the stamp in his passport with a smile that said it all.

✦

That January of 1978, he set off to America. He was as excited as I was anxious. I felt a vague alarm about where this unexpected good luck would lead. Carla's two-week tour would take in both New York and the West Coast.

Before he left, we celebrated a very odd New Year's Eve. I went to hear him play a one-off performance with glam-rocker Gary Glitter. Glitter's fortunes had begun to fade, and this was his first performance in a series of hopeful come-backs. Over his long career, that would stretch from 1972 through to the mid-1990s, Glitter would stack up twenty-six hit singles, including the iconic rock anthem, "I'm the Leader of the Gang," and his, "Rock and Roll, Part 2," which is still played at sporting events, and is greeted with the audience shouting, "Hey!"

The show was at the Rainbow Theater, not far from where we lived. I left the boys to watch the live broadcast safely at home with a babysitter. From where I sat in the theater balcony, I picked up the jolt of excitement as the psyched-up audience chanted: "Come on, come on!" when Glitter, clad in studded black leather edged with glittering silver, appeared on stage on his motorbike and charged through a hoop of fire.

I have no memory of the rest of the show, except for smiling to see Gary standing onstage, beside such an ostentatious rocker; he was, finally, upstaged. Backstage, I had the pleasure of meeting The Sex Pistol's Johnny Lydon—aka Johnny Rotten—who was there to lend support to Glitter and had brought along his mother for company. She was a cheery working-class woman, and while Gary and Mr. Glitter were mopping off the sweat, I sat chatting with her, trying to imagine my own mother sitting there. I wished there'd been something closer, tougher, more resilient, between me and my mother; something that might have created a bond that went beyond that of mother and daughter.

As for Gary Glitter, it wasn't until 1997 in America that I would read about the downward spiral in his private life, and the long list of charges for pedophilia. Fame is a dangerous condition; the price is paid one way or another, sometimes with the abuse of a rainbow of drugs, sometimes by sex in all its perversions. It is, despite all apparent advantages, lonely at the top.

◆

My husband's absence was even more wrenching this time. He was thousands of miles away and the irony was, I had made it possible for him to go. I managed to sufficiently rein in my imaginings about women that instead of wallowing in self-pity at being left alone again, I knuckled down to long hours of piano practice and singing, and listening to new music.

Kate Bush's song, "Wuthering Heights," appeared out of nowhere to console me. "You had a temper, like my jealousy... How could you leave me? When I needed to possess you? I hated you, I loved you too. Heathcliff, it's me, Cathy, come home now... It gets lonely on the other side from you." Few women, least of all me, could resist the classic Jane Brontë story of jealousy and spurned love.

When I discovered that Kate had begun composing songs at the age of thirteen, beginning with, "The Man with the Child in His Eyes," all I could think was: *who could possibly compete with that?* At thirteen, my voice had been paralyzed. Kate's songs made such an impact on me I asked Nick if I could get an hour or two in Britannia Row to put down a couple of new songs on piano. Pink Floyd had just begun recording *The Wall* which would take forever, and not be released until the end of the following year. But Nick saw to it that I got a slot.

By then I had gotten to know Nick Griffiths—the engineer who recorded the Islington Green School choir singing, "Another Brick in the Wall." In fact, I had a crush on Nick, and was sad to read a few years ago that he too died young, at fifty-three.

But it was Brian Humphries who agreed to record my session. The songs I put down were, "I'm Nobody's Angel," (an explanation or apology, perhaps?), and, "Fly like a Bird," about my ever-present need for freedom. I had no idea what I was going to do with the demos. The aim of every musician I knew was to record his or her material: it symbolized a step towards the eventual album that would bring success.

Somewhere along the way—and clearly it wasn't a major thrill as I barely remember it—one of my pop-rock songs had been heard by a producer who entered it into the Eurovision Song Contest. I vaguely recall a moment or two of excitement, waiting to hear if it had been accepted; and then no more was said about it.

✦

He came home from the States in February and it didn't take long to see that a major change had happened. His American accent was more pronounced. He was exhilarated with the music, and with the musicians he'd met and played with on both the East and West Coasts: among them were trumpeter Don Cherry, and Charlie Haden, whose album, *Liberation Music Orchestra*, was one of our favorites. He'd hung out in all the old familiar places in New York City, and had gone Upstate to record with Carla in her Grog Kill studio, near Woodstock.

"What do you think about going to live in America?" he asked me one morning a few weeks after he'd got back.

The bombshell had dropped. He hadn't said anything about living there when I got him the visa; going on tour was a very different story to uprooting us all. "I know you'd love it. And the boys would too," he said.

When I look back, I can't easily explain why I agreed to go and start a whole new life. Though the arts were still suffering from the economic downturn, we were not in dire straits. But Gary was working less at music and more at house removals so that the idea of working with Carla, of America being more affluent, seemed good reasons to take the plunge. Wanderlust was in my blood, and perhaps the neon lights and wide avenues of New York City had already worked their magic on me.

I asked the boys the same question Gary had asked me. They both said, "Ooh, yes! When do we go?" They'd heard so much about America from Gary and from their favorite TV programs that living there was an exciting prospect. Children live mostly in the moment. That they would miss their father and friends, and their survivors' camp, would come later, when the dust had settled.

As well as the change looming in our lives, I recall there being many catastrophes and major political events during that year. Egypt made peace with Israel. John Paul 1 became Pope. India had its worst monsoon ever, leaving millions homeless, and cult leader Jim Jones told nine hundred of his followers to commit suicide. The oil-tanker Cadiz ran aground off Brittany causing an ecological disaster, and an earthquake struck Iran, killing twenty thousand.

But life went on and we had much to plan for our departure to the 'New World.' We settled on the following January, 1979, ten years after he'd been deported.

I cannot remember much being said either by his parents or mine about our emigrating, mostly because it was a shock, and they couldn't grasp why we would want to leave England to live in America. For us, it was a great new family adventure.

His last gig in England was another bizarre New Year's Eve bash, this time at Guy's Hospital, for the doctors and nursing staff. I went along, to be with him, although I spent most of the evening alone, laughing at the faces he made and at the ill-matched group of musicians gathered on the make-shift stage: a young rock guitarist with a mane of untamed hair; a fresh-faced country-style bass player, and a rather elderly gentleman in a lounge suit who played drums like clockwork. Gary kept himself awake as the hours until midnight dragged on, throwing in riffs from nursery rhymes or lewd songs which the doctors and nurses were too looped to notice.

It was only a matter of days now, as we packed the things we needed to take with us to America, and set aside those we would leave behind in storage, to send on when we had got settled.

15

We arrived at John F. Kennedy airport on January 19, 1979, amid a light snowfall. It was my elder son's fourteenth birthday, and a moment neither he nor I will ever forget.

We had flown on cheap last-minute stand-by tickets, with two suitcases each and perhaps four hundred dollars in our pockets. Gary was back in his country, ready to go—"Have saxophone, will travel." We were like all America's immigrants who had left their homeland in search of a better life, whatever better meant for each of them.

We were put up by friends Gary had made on his previous visit, and wasted no time. He dashed around to see musicians and promoters, including Giorgio Gomelsky, who he'd known since his involvement with Soft Machine and Julie Driscoll. I called the only contact I had, the son of our eccentric neighbor in London—the one with the horse and donkey. He was now living in the West Village, and while he was showing me around, took me to meet Bob Guccione, Jr.

Bob was the English-educated son of Penthouse publisher, Bob Guccione, Sr., and had just been made editor-in-chief of his father's new science-fiction magazine *Omni*. Bob needed a secretary and when I told him I had secretarial skills, he offered me the job. He was into karate and loved music, so we had plenty in common besides our British humor and accents.

During the years I knew Bob, I would go with him to his father's mansion house on New York's Upper East Side where we'd be greeted in the gigantic marble entrance hall by a pair of Rhodesian ridgebacks, a Roman-style swimming pool, paintings by Picasso and Chagall, and an elevator that would take us up to the kitchen for lunch. I won't easily forget going to Bob's twenty-first birthday party and sitting at the white gilded Steinway that had once belonged to Judy Garland.

Out of the blue, within a few weeks of our arrival, we got an offer to take care of an apartment in Brooklyn Heights, while the owner was on a three-month sabbatical. From here, I started my new job, and my husband went on the road again, first with Carla's band, and then with Terry Adams' group, NRBQ.

New York is a city that never sleeps, and never stops challenging you. In the evenings, after my job and after settling the boys, I went out to jazz clubs to hear music and meet musicians—to Sweet Basil and the Village Vanguard on Seventh Avenue, and to Phoebe's on the Bowery. I was aware that the streets were not the safest place for a woman to be walking at night, but as our karate master had taught us, I was constantly vigilant.

It was hard managing alone in a new city, and a new country. And my jealousy did not disappear because we'd moved across the Atlantic. Gary was now meeting American women, who were more assertive than their English counterparts, and, therefore, I imagined, sexier too. When he did come home for a few days, our fights were more frequent; sometimes physical. I knew I was sounding like Elizabeth Taylor in *Who's Afraid of Virginia Woolf?*—spewing rage onto Richard Burton, echoing the couple's real-life marital dramas.

Everything was oversize in America—the cars, the buildings, even the servings of food. Too much was wasted, and everything was noisy, and as my mother had always said, Americans spoke too loudly. I had no choice, if I wanted to be heard, but to speak more loudly myself, although I resisted acquiring an American accent.

I enrolled the boys at school in Brooklyn, but things did not go well. They came home one afternoon to report that a boy had pulled out a knife in the playground. Another day, my younger son came home minus his anorak. He'd tried to get it back but had gotten punched for his trouble. Neither of the boys was a sissy; they'd both done their share of scrapping, but not at this level. I also discovered to my horror that they were spending all their pocket-money on junk food: Snickers and slices of pizza.

I relayed all these dramas to Gary during phone calls. Since we'd arrived, he'd been caught up in a whirlwind of music, road tours with Carla and with NRBQ. In between all this, he spent a few days recording with Carla in Grog Kill. It was from there he called me with another of his ideas: "Let's move up here! What do you say?"

"Hmm," I said. I'd just got used to my job and going out and about in New York City.

"It's beautiful in the mountains, and rents are a lot cheaper," he said.

◆

It was April, just after the last snow fall, when I drove Upstate. He had found us a log cabin for three hundred dollars a month, a few hundred yards through the woods from Carla's house. I was quite upset that he wouldn't be there when we arrived. On the way there, I looked at the miles of countryside and wondered what on earth I'd do every day, and where I'd find musicians to play with.

After buying basic food supplies in Woodstock, I drove the dozen miles on Route 212, past Cooper Lake, to Willow, and to Grog Kill Road. We found the cabin, set back off the corner of the road, on a wooded hillside. Once inside, I opened all the windows. Apart from fresh air, I soon discovered there was no electricity, gas, or water, as they hadn't been turned on. I rallied the boys and we went down to the creek to fill a bucket and saucepans with water. I lit the cabin's stove with wood from the stack outside so that we could boil the water for tea and bake potatoes for lunch. It felt like a holiday, there was no noisy traffic, it was peaceful. I took a deep breath: perhaps I could live here.

That first night, when we went to bed, my younger son, who now had his own room, called out nervously: "Mum! It's so dark! I can't see a thing!" I looked out the window, there wasn't a light anywhere .The silence and darkness were eerie; life in the woods would take some getting used to.

Me in front of our log cabin in Willow.

It is summer and we are living in the Catskill Mountains. The boys are attending Onteora High School, and are picked up each morning by a yellow school bus. Our family is more splintered now than in London. The boys hang out with their new school friends, explore the countryside—watching out for rattle snakes and bears—and are at home less often. I am more than ever a musician's widow. My piano has arrived with a shipment of furniture from England; I have had it tuned and am catching up with practicing.

He returns from a road trip. He hasn't stopped for months. As well as NRBQ, he has been a guest with Daevid Allen's group

Gong at CBGB's, and has played concerts with The Carla Bley Band at Carnegie Hall and The Public Theater. For this one, I had gone down to the City and taken the boys. When Carla saw them, she got them up on stage, and asked my fearless younger son to introduce the band—not something to be sneezed at, with fourteen or so musicians' names to remember. With a showman's sense of timing, he got all the names right.

Now, in Willow, I am at my piano downstairs, in a room with French windows that overlooks green undergrowth and tall beech trees. "What's that you're playing? I dig that!" he says. He has a full-on American accent now; he's let go of England and its English. He is tired, but he's never so tired that music doesn't grab him. I am playing a few chords with a lilting rhythm, a cross between an English hymn and an American gospel song. I tell him I'm calling it "Anglo American," and he smiles.

With time on his hands, between road trips, he is invited to teach at Karl Berger's Creative Music Studio, along with luminaries Don Cherry, Charlie Haden, Ed Blackwell, Jack DeJohnette, and U.K. visitors, Lol Coxhill and Fred Frith.

All fired up, he tells me he's asked bass-player Steve Swallow and drummer D. Sharpe to come and play. "With them, and you on piano, it'll make a nice quartet," he says. Steve is one of the most respected contemporary bass-players around. He and D. Sharpe—who will tragically die of AIDS a year later—are also members of Carla's band. It seems Gary's enthusiasm is as contagious in America as it was in England; and his confidence in me as constant.

Jim Russek, whose Brooklyn apartment we had borrowed, has become a fan of our music and offers to finance an album of the Quartet which we record in Carla's studio. The studio is quiet, amid trees and greenery. Gary enjoys every moment, forgetting the frenzy of the road. He stands in the trickling stream outside the studio, his trousers rolled up, recording a new bass clarinet version of "Ginkie," that he re-names "Round Ginkie." I'm thrilled when he chooses three of my new compositions too,

The Gary Windo Quartet at Johns Hopkins; l to r, D. Sharpe, Gary, Steve Swallow, me.

though my own sense of being a bona fide musician is now more settled. As well as "Anglo American," the other two tracks are: a repetitive little riff I call "Quick Steps," over which Steve Swallow plays a lovely lyrical bass solo, and a new version of my pop song "The Sun and the Moon," that defies definition.

Not long after we finish recording the album, which he calls *Loaded Vinyl*, I get ready for my first road tour. Gary has booked two gigs for the Gary Windo Quartet: an outdoor performance at Johns Hopkins University in Baltimore, and another in a club in Philadelphia.

There are few labels that will risk releasing such marginal material, and we don't have the time to hawk it around; consequently, as with the Britannia Row album, it does not get released.

Twenty-five years later, and twelve years after my husband's death, Cuneiform Records releases an album that includes two tracks from the Britannia Row tapes and five from Loaded Vinyl, and uses Anglo American as the title. To everyone's surprise, the BBC names it Jazz Album of the Week. Peter Marsh writes: "...Even amongst the company he kept, Gary Windo was a one-off... [Windo] specialized in a quirky fusion...of Junior Walker and Pharoah Sanders...of sweet folk ballads, cheesy rock 'n' roll and absurdist art punk songs."

There was a pause for a while in Gary's musical wanderings. We relaxed as a family in our woodland cabin, swam in the creek and lazed on the rocks. Don Preston, the keyboard player with Frank Zappa's Mothers of Invention, flew in from Los Angeles with his wife Tina, to put down some music with Carla. We met and made friends and talked endlessly of music; that we would be seeing them again before long in Los Angeles didn't enter our heads.

Steve Swallow and me.

A month or so passed in rural peace, and then, in October, Nick Mason showed up at Grog Kill studio to record a solo album. He named it *Fictitious Sports*, which I imagined was a joke about his sports car racing. Nick played drums and produced his album, but it was material written by Carla. Gary was there to provide a couple of his signature sax solos but we didn't get to see much of Nick because he was on a tight Pink Floyd schedule for the release of *The Wall*, and was gone as soon as the tracks were down.

It wasn't long before Gary too had gone. Alone again, I was

impatient to find musicians to play with. One Saturday evening, I left the boys in the log cabin watching TV and drove along the dark country road to a bar I'd heard about, a few miles away in Mount Tremper.

The White Water Depot was a barn-like place with a huge log fire. The country band was playing a number that featured slide guitar. It wasn't a scene I fit into. I ordered a Jack Daniels as nonchalantly as I could.

The owner-bartender was Billy Twigg; a friendly guy who knew what the locals wanted but was clearly a rough diamond. A few years later, he would be shot dead by Texas drug dealers. That evening, I accepted an offer to play pool with a tall shaggy-haired young man wearing the country outfit of jeans, boots and checkered shirt. His name was Richard McCarthy. At some point that evening, I told him I was getting a band together. "Sounds good to me, I play bass," he said. "And you gotta call it Pam Windo and The Shades."

It wasn't long before I had found a drummer, Chris Grassi, a great guy who had a stutter he managed like a star and that earned him the band nickname *Chawa*. Guitarist Charlie Brocco, an accomplished musician with a sharp sense of humor came next. And as I had to have a saxophone, being so used to hearing it accompany my songs, I'd already contacted Gary's old friend, Ian Bennett, who lived close by in High Falls. That made five of us in The Shades.

I was listening to a lot of new wave artists. In the pure avant-garde jazz days, I would never have thought to listen to Blondie, and was surprised to find I liked her catchy tunes, "The Tide is High," and "Heart of Glass." I steeped myself in Marianne Faithfull's, "The Ballad of Lucy Jordan," and "Working Class Hero," from her new *Broken English* album. Much later, with Hal Willner, who was producing her album, I would meet and talk to Marianne in a New York studio. And then Chrissie Hynde with The Pretenders came out with "Brass in Pocket," and both inspired and depressed me with her mesmerizingly husky voice, and her sexy lyrics. I would briefly meet Chrissie a few years on, after her show at Poughkeepsie's The Chance. I listened too to Lou Reed, my favorites, "Sweet Jane" and "Take a Walk on the Wild Side;" and, of course, there was always, Leonard Cohen. None of these artists had what could be called 'great' singing voices—one was cracked from drugs and hard living, another was a monotonous chant—but they helped me accept my own vocal limitations.

Though The Shades musicians must have wondered what they'd got themselves into, with my idiosyncratic mix of tunes, jazz chords, and chanteuse-type vocals, they rehearsed without raising an eyebrow (not that I saw anyway), or knowing where it would go. My younger son was impressed that I had myself a group but was upset because he'd harbored the notion that when I did, he'd be my drummer.

It is a sad thing, when I look back, that while our music was moving ahead, our marital arguments were increasing in frequency and intensity. He had met women in Austin, Boston and New York, and kept in touch with them; I had asked, he had told me. I'd had affairs too, with a couple of local musicians; Woodstock was in the last stages of its Hippie era. None of this had seemed to pose any more of a threat to our marriage than it had before. But it did. I have no answer as to why. Was I the saner one in the end, reacting with my rages to what was abnormal? I know now that there is nothing more powerful or more destructive than sexual jealousy. Neither of us could stop having affairs, as if they had become the substance, the raison d'être, of our union. We both held to the marriage and to our freedom; we wanted the best of both worlds. "From a certain point onward there is no longer any turning back. That is the point that must be reached," wrote Franz Kafka.

16

And then one day in October of that same year, he fell seriously ill. He called me from a hotel room in Albany, in great pain. Baxter, NRBQ's roadie, drove him all the way back to Kingston Hospital because he wanted to be near home. I was waiting and cringed when I saw him crumpled up in the car. His fast and furious lifestyle had caught up with him. His colon had ruptured; he had a serious case of peritonitis.

He was in hospital for two weeks, confined finally to lying still in bed. By the time he came out, thinner but still raring to go, I'd moved us to a house in Woodstock proper, in a secluded lane a stone's throw from where Jimi Hendrix had once stayed. The house had a large open living-room, so I could rehearse The Shades regularly. And behind the house, was a large wild pond, with a punt, so the boys would row out and check out the snapping-turtles.

The day I brought Gary home from hospital was the first time he heard the band. We played him my first 'new wave' tune, "Gimme, gimme." "That's real cool," he said, and picked up his horn. "Keep on like this and the band will be gigging soon!" I wasn't even sure what 'like this' meant, but his enthusiasm rang in my ears and I composed a half dozen more numbers.

The Creative Music Studio let us use their performance space for a session that was between a rehearsal and a gig. There may have been a few musicians and students who passed by and listened, but it was more to give the band the sense that we were a band.

Pam Windo & The Shades at the Creative Music Studio; l to r, Charlie Brocco, Gary, Ian Bennett, Richard McCarthy.

Without fully recuperating from his illness, when Carla asked if he'd join her on a European tour, Gary agreed. Nothing could stop him. The tour was a whirlwind: Berlin, Oslo, Brussels, Paris, Lyon and London. In another life, in which I would have been a proper wife, I would have insisted he stay home, and nursed him. But then he would have been a different husband.

By Christmas he was back in hospital for the last treatment. The boys and I celebrated with Woodstock friends; but it was a sad day without him. And then, released from hospital, that New Year's Eve, he got a call for a one-off gig. Like the New Year's Eve stints he'd done in London, it was an odd one, backing Tiny Tim at The White Water Depot. The six-foot tall Tiny Tim sang his "Tiptoe through the Tulips" hit in his funny falsetto voice, accompanying himself on ukulele, while Gary threw in a selection of sax riffs and grinned the whole way through.

I was now caught up in a frenzy preparing The Shades for our debut gig. By then, without any real discussion, Gary had assigned himself my bandmaster, and threw himself into song arrangements and staging. He worked out sassy saxophone fills and duets that he and Ian would play side by side, taking turns to play solos. Why he did all this, I did not question then, but now I wonder: had Carla's band taken a break from touring? Or did NRBQ have less frequent gigs? Or, perhaps, with more space and freedom than with their bands, he could now go the whole hog?

Pam Windo and The Shades performed its first gig in March of 1980. Naturally, I chose The White Water Depot, ignoring the fact I was bringing a New Wave-Punk band to a country bar where the locals were folk and blues junkies. I wore a scarlet satin jacket and tight black pants. Leslie Gerber, the Woodstock Times' music critic, wrote: "...a startlingly effective debut...a tonic for the sinuses...despite only having enough material for one set."

Johanan Vigoda, lawyer to Stevie Wonder, was in the audience that night and was overheard by a friend to remark that I had "star quality." All of which naturally propelled me onwards.

As my confidence gathered momentum, I was composing more and more songs for The Shades' repertoire and by April we were back at the Depot with two sets, for a four-day booking we called *The White Water Depot Hijack*. For this, Gary constructed an enormous pair of pink shades to hang over the band, and made colorful collage posters, telling everyone to come wearing their own shades, which he pasted up all around town.

The hijack evenings were a success: the country music fans were joined by the Punk converts—all of them wearing shades— who jumped up and down pogo-style to show their approval. Reviews this time were mixed, but most marveled at my spunk

Gary's collage poster for a Pam Windo and The Shades gig.

and energy, and my provocative offbeat lyrics. I was even called a "bitch goddess," and an "outside pianist, even by Carla Bley's standards."

There was much celebrating the last night of the hijack: during the last set, the drummer's wife gave birth to a baby boy. When the phone call came with the news, Chris leaped up in the air from his drum-stool with a loud "Yeah!" and Billy Twigg popped a bottle of champagne.

During the four-day 'hijacking,' a journalist came to interview me. The next day, an article and photo of the band appeared on the front page of The Kingston Times, beneath the lead story about the Iran hostages.

The Shades were on a roll. The week before my next gig, I was sitting at the bar of the Little Bear Chinese restaurant, passing the time with some musician buddies.

There was always someone around; among our Woodstock friends and neighbors were Mick Ronson, Eric Andersen, Robbie Dupree, Johnny Average, Tom Pacheco, and John Sebastian. Rick Danko and Levon Helm still lived there too. Rick would later sit in with The Shades on a snowy winter's night at the White Water Depot, where, perhaps to help the audience forget the cold, he counted us in to play "Sea Cruise." Later, too, I would go with a friend to meet Levon Helm at his studio.

Paul Butterfield was another neighbor, at the time signed to Albert Grossman, and touring with Rick Danko as the Danko-Butterfield Band. Gary, who continued to conjure up musicians, had brought Paul to our house one day, where he'd played a few bars of blues on my funky piano. For Gary, it was full circle: years before, when he was first paying his dues in America, he had played a gig with The Paul Butterfield Blues Band.

That afternoon, Albert happened to walk into the bar. He sat down at the far end, and I gave him a quick glance. I'd seen him around, but he liked to keep a low profile. He was a tall, hefty and distinguished-looking man who wore a daily uniform of Levi

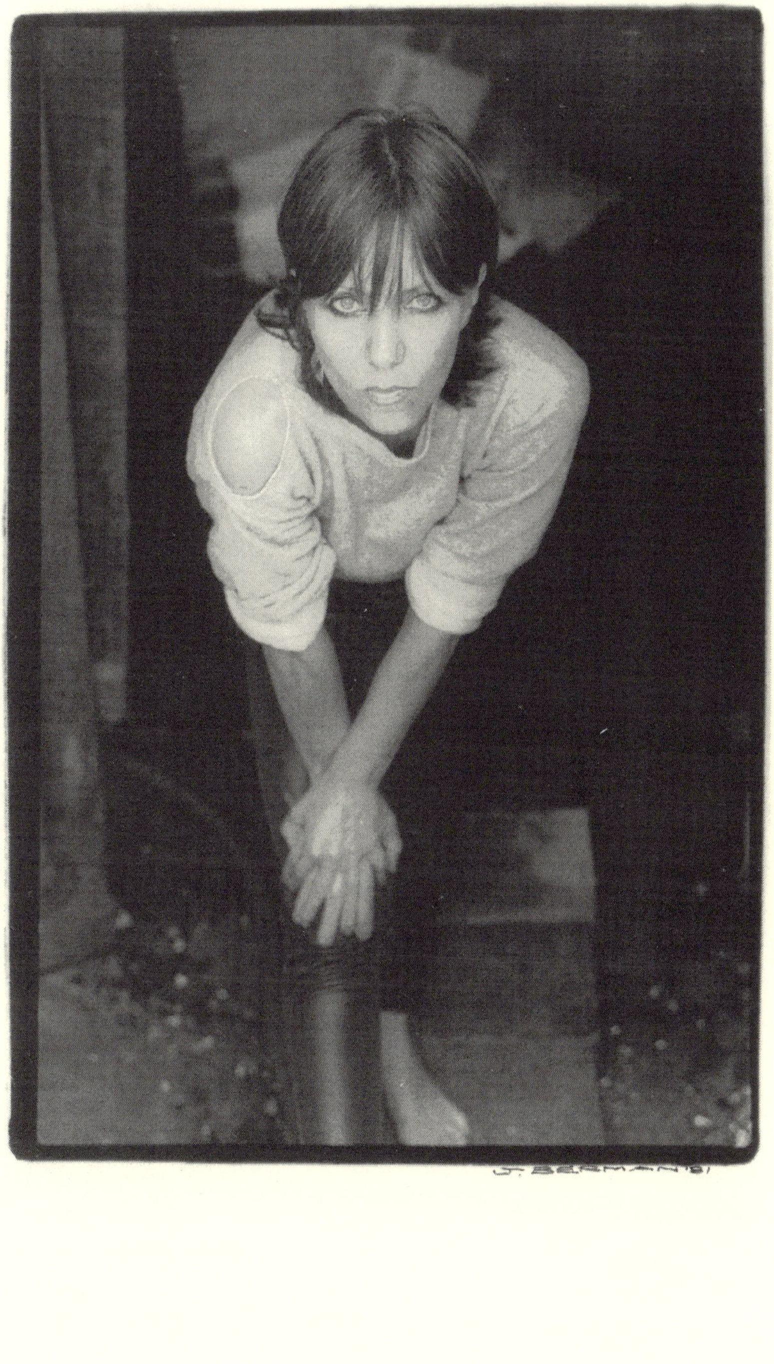
J. BERMAN '81

Albert Grossman caught up close and smiling.

jeans, white South American alpaca shirt and deck shoes. He had a large pink face, straggly white hair pulled back into a pony-tail, and his piercing blue eyes watched the world from behind round wire-rimmed spectacles.

    Albert had discovered and managed Bob Dylan, Janis Joplin, Peter, Paul and Mary, and Todd Rundgren, among others. He owned the Little Bear restaurant, along with the Big Bear restaurant next door; the Bearsville Theater next to the restaurant (behind which he would later be buried), as well as Bearsville Studios and Bearsville Records. In short, he all but owned Bearsville, and when he walked in, everyone knew it.

I was wearing skintight pants and a grey sweatshirt ripped open on the shoulder. My hair was cut short, and was dyed with red henna. I was laughing with the guys, feeling ready for something good. Albert looked over and signaled to the bartender to pour me a drink. I smiled and went to sit next to him. He wasn't there for small-talk so I did the obvious and told him about my band, that we were performing the following Saturday, and wouldn't he come and see us?

When Albert showed up for the gig, Gary was out front, checking the stage. He ran back to the make-shift dressing room, shouting, "Albert's here!" He had the benefit of years of performing, but the guys in my band looked, and were, as nervous as I was to hear the big shot had come.

I stood up front at microphone, trying not to show how terrified I was, and trying to forget Albert Grossman was in the audience. I was wearing a man's white shirt drawn in at the waist with a black studded belt; a pair of glittery bikini panties; black stockings held up by a visible black garter belt, and a pair of stiletto shoes. On stage, I felt Gary watching me, as if he couldn't believe his eyes, seeing me strutting around and chanting, "I want your body, to hell with your mind, 'cos I've got a mind of my own." And while he played a solo, I was running my hands up and down his legs, with a rose clenched between my teeth.

After a good deal of applause and whistling, I went straight into the next number—"Waiting for you is boring. Do you do it to be annoying?"—during which I acted out being angry, going to the piano and thumping the keys with my fists and elbows, while the musicians playacted at ignoring me.

The enigmatic Daevid Allen, was either at that gig, or somehow heard of this number, and would tell me later that he'd immediately written a song in response, which he called: "Keeping you waiting is exciting!"

Albert must have liked something he heard and saw because when we finished performing, he came back to the dressing-room. A man from the audience was begging me to sign the lining of his jacket with the words, "Fuck you," and kept saying, "You were great!" While I was trying to figure out how this could be happening to me, Albert cut in. "Okay, guys," he said, in his deep voice, eyeing my legs. "I want to talk to the lady in the garter belt. Would you leave us alone, please?"

When they'd all filed out, including a reluctant Gary,

Me at a gig, The White Water Depot.
Photo by Gary Gershoff

Albert said, "I think we can do something. Come to my office next week and we'll talk." And then he left.

◆

I went to see him and he offered me a recording contract. I would be signed to the Bearsville label, and in exchange he would give me twenty thousand dollars. A few days before my thirty-eighth birthday, in that May of 1980, I agreed and he handed me the check. It was a mind-blowing moment, as if I was being rewarded, paid in arrears, for the ten years of penniless struggles I'd gone through to get to this moment. We held a big party to celebrate; all of us—Gary and I, and the musicians—imagining we were on our way to the big time. I dismissed what I knew only too well: that my age put me at a disadvantage. But I still had the energy of a performer—as well as the looks—and had finally found enough of a voice for what I wanted to express. I dismissed, too, the fact that I'd got a record deal too soon; before, as bandleader, I'd known the direction I was going in, and before my band had had the chance to stretch out and find its sound. Gary saw what he thought it could be, and had got us quickly on the road.

Albert arranged to fly the band to Los Angeles to perform a showcase for Warner Brothers at the Whisky a Go Go. He needed Warner's go-ahead to record an album in his studio, as they distributed his artists. Just before we left, we'd had to let Richard go and find a new bass-player. Ed Fitzgerald came

The Whisky a Go Go billboard.

recommended, cut his long hair to fit in with the band's 'look,' and had a hectic week getting the numbers down for the show.

When the limo drove us along Sunset Boulevard to take in the sights before the performance, I noticed that the Whisky a Go Go's billboard had put a 'w' at the end of my name. Janis Joplin had sung at the Whisky; she wouldn't have taken that without a fuss, so I made a fuss, and the 'w' was removed. We were booked into famous digs too, in the Chateau Marmont, and were given bungalow Number Three. Two years later, John Belushi would die from a drug overdose in that same bungalow.

Before the show, Warner Bros make-up department hauled me in and did such a number on my face—a very glamorous pop-star one—that my musicians barely recognized me. Afterwards, the A&R man clasped my hand, leaving a tiny package in it that turned out to contain cocaine. I did not know that he had done the same with all the band members. The bass player, Ed, knew nothing of such delights, and forgot what key the first number was in.

I started the show with Wilson Pickett's "I'm a Midnight Mover," a suitably sexy standard, before I went into my own quirky numbers. I had not seen that the piano stool was out of place and when I made the planned high kick as I went into the song my shoe got caught on it and was catapulted into the audience. I was about to throw off the other shoe so I wouldn't be hobbling around, when a man from the audience placed the lost one back on the stage. I put it on, and carried on. Warner's people thought I'd done it intentionally for shock effect, as they no doubt did when Ed kicked the amp he'd been provided with off the stage with a loud "This is a piece of shit!"

On the plane to Los Angeles, Albert had handed me a small package. "For good luck," he'd said, quite matter-of-fact. It was a band of feathers Janis Joplin had worn in her hair. Albert was at the tail end of his fabulously successful career as show-biz impresario, and had hoped perhaps to have one last success

BIO

PAM WINDO AND THE SHADES

<u>I want your body</u> ©1980
<u>To hell with your mind</u> ©1980
<u>I've got a mind of my own</u> ©1980

Pam Windo is The Liberated Woman. Pam Windo is unabashed punk. Pam Windo is spearheading a new Underground. Pam Windo is flashes of Cabaret, old Berlin, Berthold Brecht, Kurt Weil and Marlene Dietrich's legs. Pam Windo is a magician, pulling mystique out of thin air like she was slipping a nylon mesh up her thigh. Is she Berlin or Brighton, England, the chilly seaside resort, where she was born? She's lived in Berlin, too. She's met Mack the Knife.

Look at Pam's peekaboo slit skirts and you get the deja vu of Marlene Dietrich. Pam knows how to use her legs. She danced well enough to make her parents boast about it but they were too middle class to allow her to become a professional dancer.

<u>How much of me can I afford to give you?</u> ©1980
<u>How much of you can I expect to take?</u> ©1980
<u>How much of me can I afford to give you?</u> ©1980
<u>How much of you can I expect to take?</u> ©1980

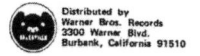

Distributed by
Warner Bros. Records
3300 Warner Blvd.
Burbank, California 91510

Warner Bros' bio.

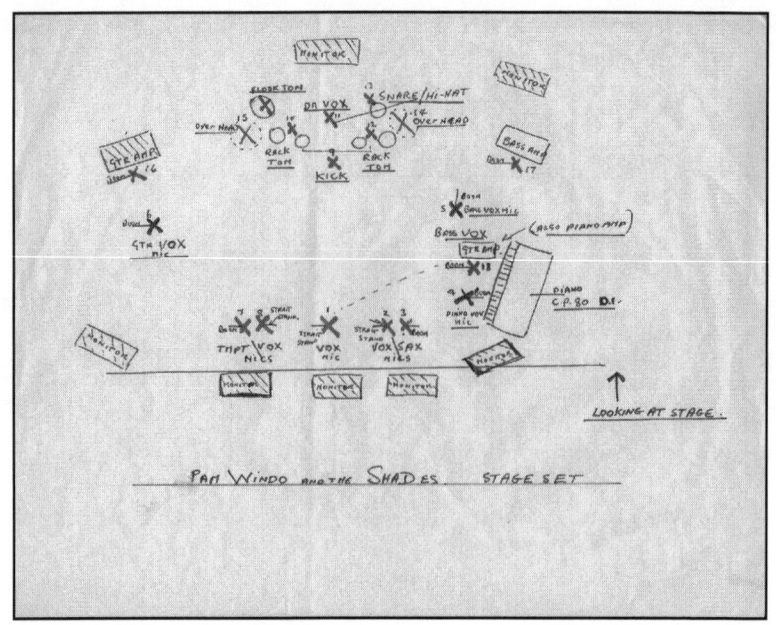

Gary's sketch for the stage set.

in me. But it isn't just luck, or charm, or even talent that brings success: a combination of all three is a good bet. For the rest, it will always be a mystery.

Warner Bros gave Albert the go-ahead. Gary was as excited that we were going to record an album in Bearsville Studio as he'd been in Britannia Row, and to give the project the importance it deserved, he wrote up a track listing, this time on the inside of a Kellogg's Cornflakes box, illustrating it with cartoon faces and expletives.

We spent several weeks recording, which I found grueling. During this time, though I sensed I had lost control of whatever vision and sound I had originally had for my music, I got as caught up as everyone else in the intensity and excitement of it all—songs I had written in a slow rhythm got faster; vocals that, alone, I sang quietly, got louder.

When we'd completed all the tracks, Albert sent us, along

with the band's manager, Ian Kimmet, to Miami, to mix the album. He also gave us the keys to his Coconut Grove house, complete with swimming pool, where we resided for the duration, and where the boys hung out while we were at work.

When it was all done, Albert chose the album's title, *It*. I never understood why. He hired a top PR company, and found me a backer-manager. This is from the PR's press release: "Pam's stage spectacle, the cutting edge of her lyrics, and the tight precision of the band with Gary as concertmaster... Pam sings the emotions of a woman seeking artistic realization in a male

Warner Bros' promo photograph.

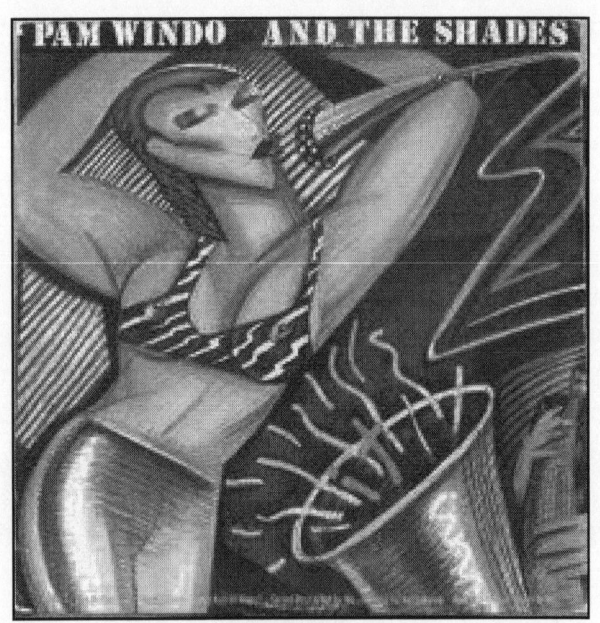

IT: *Pam Windo & The Shades album.*

world. The music is definitely new wave brass-rock. The show will stun you."

With all of this, I knew I was being pushed into the race for a hit song. Though I came close—and was even offered a song-writing contract by Warner's, which I foolishly turned down—a hit did not materialize. Some of my lyrics were catchy, and were even 'borrowed' by a couple of well-known singers; an annoyance that could not be remedied, because as Albert said when I went to him, their names and fame were greater than mine. Apart from the pressure of finding a hit, a formula I did not have the inclination to fathom, I was having fun with the band. There were endless photo shoots by well-known photographers, which made us all feel like rock stars, and we had the use of Albert's vintage black limo, as well as a big old barn to rehearse in whenever we wanted. On stage, I forgot everything but entertaining the audience.

◆

It was about then, outside the Sunflower Health Food store in Woodstock that I bumped into Howard Johnnson, a well-known jazz tuba-player. He told me, in a cryptic confiding manner: *'You have no idea what a big influence you've been in the music world.'* He was right, I had no idea what he meant, and it was obvious he wasn't about to explain himself. He quickly moved on to say that he had recently spoken to John Lennon and Yoko Ono—he was recording tuba parts on their *Double Fantasy* album—about Gary's talent in arranging saxophone parts, and added that he'd even proposed him for their album tour. A few days before the date that was fixed for Howard to introduce Gary, John was assassinated.

Promo shot of The Shades, l to r, Ian Bennett, Charlie Brocco, Ed Fitzgerald, Chris Grassi, Gary and me.

Just this year, by chance, as I was writing, I came across an interview that Howard had given to the online magazine *Roll*. In it, he revealed something else: *"I spoke to him [John] the night he died. I was going to bring John and Yoko a recording I had of Pam Windo—she's married to a saxophone player named Gary Windo and she sang, frankly, something like Yoko did. She and her husband and another tenor player... had a way of playing unison parts —the same notes but having it sound very strange because the pitches were dirty on one or both of them but their phrasing was exactly right. So it just ended up being a great sound that I thought John would like because these guys could also play in tune and John had talked to me about taking a horn section on tour. So I called the studio. Yoko answered the phone and passed it to John. I said, 'I brought that record with the tenor players I'd like you to hear, should I bring it up to the studio?' And he said, 'We're going to leave a little early tonight, bring it in tomorrow in the afternoon.' And I thought, 'Well, that's good' because I wanted to watch Monday night football. And Monday night football is what told us that he had been killed."*

I cannot help but wonder now how I would have felt had I known this back then; and what might have happened for Gary, if John had lived.

I did, however, four years hence, find my band listed in the 1984 editions of *Who's Who in Rock Music* and *The Rolling Stone Record Guide*.

◆

I have been writing this book for several months now. People ask me how I can remember so many things from those years. So much remains vivid in my memory because we did not live in a routine way but were like those artists who go through periods of dramatic experimentation, in colors and sizes and forms, creating and re-creating themselves and their art.

But it has become even more difficult now, because it was—and still is—so painful, to write about the next few years. Just as our musical careers seemed to be peaking, our marriage began crumbling apart.

I tenaciously carried on composing and performing—as well as venues in Woodstock, we appeared at Poughkeepsie's The Chance, New York's CBGB's, and at Studio 54. Between Gary and Albert, and the band members, there were too many opinions being thrown in the mix. With the pressure to be successful, to live up to Albert's bet on me, I was acting out—shouting, stamping, even throwing stiletto shoes across the studio. I was 'the point,' the front man of the band, it all fell on me. And so this show-off behavior became my life. My musicians, though they did among themselves, never complained to me.

Albert watched, taking it all in, and insisted I change all my original musicians, believing they were the reason I was not as successful as he'd hoped. Guitarist John Platania, who'd played and recorded with Van Morrison, joined us, as did Ron Riddle, who'd been associated with The Cars. John Marsh, a bass-player from Chicago, came in recommended by Ron. It was a steaming band and to match the sound, we dressed in ever more outrageous stage get-ups. Gary grew his hair long and bleached it platinum blonde, he wore combat pants with a tank top, and borrowed one of my red feather ear-rings for his left ear. We made demo after demo of the songs I kept composing, in the hope of a hit. Our musical collaboration had taken over from our marriage, which we clung to without ever discussing it.

◆

At The Chance, Poughkeepsie, used on Anglo American album cover. left to right: Tedd Orr, Me, Gary, John Marsh

Gary turned blond, with The Shades at The Chance.

During the last summer we spent together, I knew he was as deeply saddened as I was that we had become estranged as man and wife. There was an unspoken recognition that everything was winding down, coming to its inevitable end. We had both continued our affairs ad nauseam; the marriage had become so 'open,' it barely existed. Through all the affairs, I had known he would not leave me nor me, him. And this is the hardest part to write: while he had kept his desire for me through all his affairs, my desire for him had left me. He had tried everything to pull me back. But it was beyond me to put this right.

There was too much happening and too much emotion for me to recall the chronology. He was now forty-one and I was forty. Although we were still involved together in The Shades— by then, mostly recording demos—we were rarely home together. I changed some of the musicians, yet again—guitarists Ted Orr and Robert Gelles took over at various times, and British bass-player Steve York, who'd recorded with Marianne Faithfull and Joan Armatrading, and who Gary had known in London, stepped in for a while too. One evening, up at Bearsville Studios, I came across Robert Fripp. We got talking and I asked if he'd listen to a demo tape. He did, and returned it with the astute comment: "Your lyrics are much better than your music," an observation that I only truly heard some years later.

I knew when heroin got a hold of him again: people told me. He took to hanging out with Rick Danko, the two of them using together. And by accident, I saw him shooting up at another musician's house. By this time, he had become closely involved with music producer Hal Willner; the two joined forces to record an album, which Gary insisted on calling *Dogface*, using tracks from different line-ups of The Shades, as well as NRBQ, and giving all the tracks 'doggy' titles.

At the time, I found this empathy with dogs and bones odd, especially since it had never emerged when we were together. We'd never owned a dog. I am sad to say that this inclination, together with the little dog Oliver, his companion in his last years, was a measure of the loneliness he was experiencing. As we drew further apart, I watched him from a distance. Even with (or perhaps because of) his addiction, musically he seemed more energetic than ever.

And then, one day, in the summer of 1982, he called me. I was in Woodstock, at a performance of my younger son's band,

A photo taken in a deserted swimming pool by Tony Wright.

At a gig.

Paris Plus.

"I have something to tell you," he said over the phone, hesitating before going on, "I'm going to leave you." There was resignation in his voice, as there had been years before, when he'd announced his first infidelity. He had again said what I already knew: my last illusion, that we would grow old and grey together, was shattered.

He told me he was in New York at Hal Willner's apartment. I recall asking my younger son, should I drive down and see him; meaning, should I try to save the marriage?

He opened the door and brought me inside. I saw him in that moment as someone separate, no longer part of the 'us' we had created. I cried for what must have been hours, for everything it had and hadn't been, until my eyes were so swollen, I could barely see. I may have loved him most in those awful moments. He held me, made me a drink, and told me about the young woman I'd heard he was seeing. I insisted on calling her several times to express my outrage. He watched, mesmerized by my breakdown, as if he hadn't expected any such thing. "She makes love just like a woman... But she breaks just like a little girl," Bob Dylan's lyrics told the story.

I shall record only snippets now. The screaming and yelling, the blind anger, the refusal to see the awful truth—that our marriage and all that it had encompassed, was over—all this I have committed to a place best kept to me alone. Most couples scream the same oaths, swear the same blame and feel hate and loathing; it is part of the death agony of a long marriage.

We had no savings and were broke. I looked around Woodstock for work to pay the rent and did some waitressing. A retired judge hired me as his part-time secretary and made it his business to help me update my skills, including lessons on the first huge word processor. At the end of the day, he would sit me down by the log fire, hand me a whisky, and say: "Now let's talk about your life." The judge was my guardian angel, and had come at just the right moment, to watch over me while I made the leap from one life to another.

I stayed on in the house with the boys while Gary went to live on a barge in a backwater of the Hudson River, where he helped the owner with maintenance, including diving to repair the hull. Sometimes I went over with a mutual friend, Joel

Drummer, Ron Riddle, not visible in the photo at The Chance.

Tornabene, a one-off big-hearted character, if ever there was one, who'd been involved with Timothy Leary back in the acid days.

Gary came back and forth to our house, and went back and forth to New York City for gigs. Through Todd Rundgren, he met the English rockers, The Psychedelic Furs, who'd had a huge hit song, "Pretty in Pink." Along with his friend, Woodstock resident and cellist, Ann Sheldon, who would tragically die in a car accident two years later, in late 1984, he was invited to record on The Furs' next hit, "Love My Way," and to go on tour with them to promote their album, *Forever Now*. We spent that Christmas of 1982 with Furs' guitarist John Ashton and his wife at our house in Woodstock. Despite recordings and concerts, we were all poor and had a make-shift sort of Christmas drinking eggnog and playing scrabble—a gathering that was to be our last as a family.

He came with me when my elder son Simon graduated from Onteora High School in 1983, for which occasion he smoked his first and only cigar. Simon had already veered away from the music that had engulfed him and had developed instead a love of landscape and the outdoors. He eventually took up photography, of landscape and people, and made a successful career of it, with travel books and articles about countries as far apart as New Zealand, Malaysia, Morocco, Ireland, and Haiti.

There was no cigar when my younger son, Jamie, graduated a year later. Jamie had already flung himself into music, as drummer in Paris Plus, a local band he co-founded. When the group played Woodstock's The Joyous Lake, Gary sat in as guest to encourage them. He went on to join the Gary Windo Band as drummer for many New York gigs. In later years, he added design work to music, doing window displays at Bergdorf Goodman, and assisting milliner Philip Treacy with his hat shows, in addition to performing his music everywhere.

My sons and I left Woodstock to make new homes in New York

City, our original port of entry. I found a place near Gramercy Park; my sons went to live in Fort Greene. The judge decided I was ready for a full-blown job in a law firm, which meant a hundred and eighty-degree flip from my previous life-style. The thought of working in an office seemed like a nightmare about to happen.

Despite my shag-cut hair, bleached platinum on top and dark below, and my very un-corporate clothes, I managed to get myself hired. The senior partner with whom I interviewed, bored senseless by his job, found me 'interesting.'

The nine-to-five job brought in enough to pay the rent and save a little. I kept up piano and rehearsed with a friend, Paul Ganz, who had played keyboards with Carly Simon and with Meat Loaf. Paul was game enough to work with me for a while on what I thought might be a piano-bar duet. I was still holding on to the past, but it didn't take me long to see that that was not to be either.

Despite the prestigious gigs and connections, Gary took a job at International Woodwind & Brass, the well-known musical instrument store in New York's midtown music hub. I don't know if he saw the irony, that he was repeating his father's early apprenticeship. He seemed to take it in stride, going between performances with celebrities and helping customers. He took to answering the store phone, "Hello. International House of Pancakes here. Can I help you?" He had perfected the art of self-mockery, the recourse of all comedians.

Concerning the end of our marriage, I felt a great rage that this unacceptable event had happened. I poured the pain, frustration, and outrage into letters, blaming him; denying my role. Despite my anger—and his sadness—as people do, when they have loved and lived together, we kept in touch. We would speak on the phone, long conversations late at night. I can still hear his voice as he calmed me down. In time, we would meet. It was impossible not to; we had known each other for more than forty years. We would eat sushi in the East Village and talk about life, music, and the boys.

 I began to write a diary, to jot notes and ideas; soon, writing song lyrics turned into writing poems. I knew then that I wanted to write. After a three-month course at New York University, my first essay was published by the *Village Voice*. I got paid five hundred dollars, and with this, decided that my career as a writer had been launched.

Again, here, I can barely remember what I did, let alone what Gary was doing, in chronological order. But I do recall very clearly that one day, when I had gone to see him at the music store, we went for lunch, and he told me he had taken up gliding. He seemed thrilled about this new adventure, and I recalled the young boy I'd known, eager to be a pilot like his father, finally taking off into the skies.

 I imagined him finding solace, alone in the sky, where he no longer felt the need to be the entertainer, or the lover. He told my younger son he was ready to do higher-level things, loop de loops and barrel rolls and had plans to go up with his teacher in a single-engine plane. He was looking forward to it as the next step toward pilot certification and a license.

 I could not keep abreast with all that Gary was doing, with my head in my writing, and my law office job. But he would call to tell me of certain things, and invite me to come along.

 In October of 1985, Gary's friend Todd Rundgren invited him to join his eleven-voice *A Cappella* Orchestra. Before their road tour, I went to a performance at The Beacon. I sat alone, and was taken back all those years to when I'd sat alone in London, at The Lyceum, hearing him play for the first time in a theater. He was no longer the stranger I'd seen him as then; but so familiar, with all his talent and craziness, that I couldn't stop the flow of tears.

◆

The years from 1986 on were bumpy for me, and for him. While I had bowed out of the music business and was working hard at my job and my writing, he was even more immersed in his music. Sometime in 1987, he took off for a visit to Los Angeles, where he did some demo tracks with our friend Don Preston. In San Francisco, with his usual flair, he hooked up with the rock band, The Tubes. He'd met vocalist Fee Waybill in Woodstock with Todd Rundgren, and went on to play several guest appearances with the band. Unlikely as it seems—although nothing was unlikely with Gary—he was introduced to Eddie Murphy, and played a gig with him. Another avant-garde band after his own heart was The Residents; whose black and white t-shirt he proudly wore.

He had by now formed his own group, the Gary Windo Band, with Knox Chandler, a brilliant young guitarist. Together they would play The Bottom Line, go on tour, and then compose the tracks for an album he called, *Deep Water;* a style of music he would call: *rock-a-bop-a-metaldelic*.

By 1988, I had no choice but to file for divorce. Gary's special visa had long since expired, and with it, mine. An American friend offered me marriage so the boys and I could live legally in the United States.

Not long after the divorce, Gary married the young Irish Catholic. For their wedding, he wore a shiny lime-green suit, and flipped his bleached-blond hair into an Elvis wave. After the ceremony, the couple jumped into the '67 Mercury Cougar convertible he'd bought on a trip to Los Angeles. He was finally living his rock 'n' roll fantasy, the one he'd only half lived back then. He'd got his car and his girl and was king of the road.

But heroin had taken over both their lives. To pay for their addiction, I knew that his wife was acting in porn movies and that Gary was composing music for the soundtracks.

He was playing gigs with his own band, and for a year or two my younger son was the drummer, playing at The Bottom Line, and The Knitting Factory, in New York City. Bookings and performances with other artists began to dwindle. By sheer willpower, he was still working at the music store, and had several students to whom he was teaching saxophone.

I would see him now and again and though he always acted like his old cheerful self, the act was less credible; as if he were deliberately presenting a caricature of his former self. My sons and I tried an intervention at his home in New York's East Village. We left, knowing it was too late.

Within a year, he called me. "Could you help with some cash? And any chance of a bed for the night?" They arrived in a car—not the convertible, which he had had to sell—that was full to the brim with their belongings. They were homeless. I fed them; they stayed the night, and I gave him a hundred dollars the next day when they set off, I knew not where.

I wasn't there to see or hear the rest. In March of 1989, I took a three-month sabbatical from my job at the law firm and went to Morocco, thinking I would write a book. When the three months were up, I went home, quit my job, put my belongings in storage and returned to live in Marrakech, for what would be another seven years. It was, without my knowing, a pilgrimage; a place to forget all that had gone before, to listen and learn from a different culture.

In those first years in Morocco, I was not in touch with him. I knew he could not hold back the demon addiction; that he was not his old self, or rather, no longer the man I had known all those years. But I was not my old self either, and could not help him back.

I did hear from my sons that Allen Ginsberg had invited him to play on his album, *The Lion for Real*, produced by Hal Willner. Gary composed the music for the title track, and thought up the name for it. That album would be the Beat poet's last recorded work before his own passing.

Just before Gary died in July of 1992, he was touring again with

Gary with Allen Ginsberg, recording The Lion for Real.

NRBQ, this time on the West Coast. It was a gig at Slim's in San Francisco that would be his last performance.

In his time, he had become a saxophone cult hero, leaving traces of his virtuosity in every kind of music. I'd been sitting with him during an interview back in 1979, after the gig we'd played at Johns Hopkins University, when he'd said: "I can love other people's playing, but I really like what I'm working on, it's like being a research chemist. Sort of like being onto a discovery... it's my journey and I'm gonna do it now." I was there, most of the time, watching him make that journey.

Though a lesser player in the starry firmament of jazz, he was not alone in coming to an untimely end. Many of his musical heroes were among the casualties: Charlie Parker made it only to age thirty-four, dying in a New York hotel of a multitude of illnesses. Charlie Mingus died at fifty-six in Mexico; his ashes were scattered in the Ganges. Albert Ayler was found dead in the East River, an apparent suicide, also at the age of thirty-four.

And Eric Dolphy died of a diabetic seizure in a Berlin hotel room aged thirty-six.

I have come to the end of this book. It has been a prolonged labor of love, of sorting through numberless memories, and laying things to rest. My memories of him reside as much in my body as in my thoughts. Only last year I dreamed he sat up in his coffin and reached out to take my hand; I felt it, soft and warm and loving.

He had walked into my life in 1969. Together, we had lived through an era of music, of new self-awareness, and of boundless, and guiltless, sexuality that was so powerful and extraordinary it could never be repeated. I watched that era morph into a rampant singles-bar scene, epitomized in the book and film, *Looking for Mr. Goodbar*. Ironically, a year or two after our sad separation, I would briefly date the husband of Judith Rossner, the author of that landmark book.

All those years with him, while I was learning to become myself, he was such a clearly defined person. Compared to him, I had a shifting personality, like a butterfly or a chameleon, born to change my colors, depending on whom I was with and where I was. The actress Jane Birkin, years after her notorious sexual escapades with a series of French men, admitted: "The truth is I did all those things to please the men I liked at the time."

Nowadays, I feel firmly myself, though I know I borrowed a great deal from him. I regret not knowing the end was near, and not seeing him again before he died. I regret not writing a heartfelt letter. I would like to tell him how much he gave me, and affected my life, and influenced the way I am living today. We rarely say the things we want to or should, before someone dies, as if we fear breaking the spell or changing the status quo, as if saying them would turn into something far worse. My sons miss him; where some mourn deeply at the time of death, their mourning is a continual daily prayer, as is mine. At their biological father's funeral, my elder son told the mourners how lucky he and his brother had been to have had *two* wonderful fathers.

In our crazy innocent way, he and I were children of our time. Even in our innocence, we were deadly serious, about life and love and music. We loved each other very much, and shared a bond beyond our ken. In writing this, I have been drawn back into the world he led me into. I could not have lived in it without him. I used to think he could have lived in it without me, but I see now that he wasn't made like that either.

It is a symptom of aging that we look back with nostalgia at our youth and claim that things were better then: 'those were the days,' and, 'the good old days.' But the Sixties and Seventies were truly an era apart, a one-off moment of cultural liberation. That we met up with all those musicians; played all those gigs, and recorded all that music with only the barest use of technology, is hard to fathom. "You don't miss what you never had," explains it in part. That we were endlessly resourceful explains the other part. There was no 'virtual reality' for us; we lived slap-bang in the moment, with all the risks and dangers, in our music and in our relationships.

✦

He took great pleasure in looking at me playing piano while he played saxophone. His mouth would be tight over the embouchure, notes pouring out, his hazel eyes shining intensely, taking everything in and sending me signals when he liked what I was playing, or meant me to take a solo.

His favorite thing when playing a humdrum pick-up gig was to break forth into a chintzy pop song like "Volare" or "Girl from Ipanema," moving his eyebrows up and down like Groucho Marx.

One summer night in New York City, when my apartment windows were opened wide, I was playing chords from a songbook—old-fashioned tunes, a soothing way to escape rock 'n' roll—when I heard a saxophone take up the melody somewhere in the street. I went to the window, thinking it was him, that he had passed by and heard me. The player was just a lonely shadow in a dark doorway.

I have at last come to the end of this book, and must let it go now so that I can continue my life. Last night, as if to help me, I dreamed it all: those years were all encapsulated, passing in front of my sleeping eyes. He was playing, on the road with musicians I did not know. There were two women he had been with. I was angry. He was angry with me too, though I didn't know why and he didn't tell me. In abbreviated dreamtime, I felt the rift and the sad separation. And then he was on stage, alone in the dark, singing, and I stepped up to join him. Our bodies were as one; our heads and hearts close together. I could hear his voice, and began to sing in harmony, very softly, following his melody. There were no instruments between us, just pure music and love.

GARY'S CONCERTS AND PERFORMANCES

Sun Festival, Roundhouse, London, 1970
Centipede, Lyceum Theatre, London, 1970
Centipede, Bordeaux, France, 1970
Symbiosis, BBC Top Gear Live Session, London, 1971
Symbiosis, Roundhouse, London, 1971
Symbiosis, Ronnie Scott's Jazz Club, London, 1971
Centipede, Lanchester Arts College, 1971
Centipede, Royal Albert Hall, London, 1971
Brotherhood of Breath, Bremen, Berlin, 1971
Symbiosis, Hammerveld Jazz Festival, Holland, 1971
Symbiosis Supersession, Goldsmith College, London, 1971
Symbiosis, Bedford College, London, 1971
Spear, Country Club, London, 1971
Louis Moholo Sextet, Bedford College, London, 1971
Alan Shorter Quartet, La Maison de la Radio, Paris, 1971
Brotherhood of Breath, Country Club, London, 1971
Brotherhood of Breath, 100 Club, London, 1971
Centipede, Rotterdam, Holland, 1972
Ray Russell's The Running Man, London, 1972
Brotherhood of Breath, Berlin Philharmonic Hall, 1972
WMWM, BBC Jazz Workshop, 1973
Brotherhood of Breath, Bremen, Willisau, Germany, 1973
Brotherhood of Breath, Queen Elizabeth Hall, London, 1973
Doris Troy Band, Tabarka Festival, Tunisia, 1974
Robert Wyatt, Drury Lane Theater, London, 1974
Centipede, Nancy, Lyons, France, 1975
Gary Windo and Friends, Maidstone College of Art, 1975
Gary and Pam Windo Duo, Maidstone College of Art, 1975
Gary Windo Quartet, Maidstone College of Art, 1975
Louis Moholo's Culture Shock, 100 Club, 1976
Carla Bley Band, Baden-Baden Workshop Orchestra, German Radio & TV, 1976
Carla Bley Band, European Tour, 1977

Carla Bley Band, Rome Festival, Italy, 1978
Carla Bley Band, Vienna Jazz Festival, Austria, 1978
Carla Bley Band, Bottom Line, New York, 1978
Carla Bley Band, UCLA, California, 1979
Charlie Haden Liberation Orchestra, San Francisco, 1979
Gary Windo and Friends, Johns Hopkins University, 1979
Carla Bley Band, US and European tours, 1978-1982
Carla Bley Band, Carnegie Hall, 1979
Carla Bley Band, Public Theater, NYC, 1979
Charlie Haden's Liberation Orchestra, San Francisco, 1979
Gary Windo Band, Boston, 1979
Gong, CBGB's, New York, 1979
NRBQ, East Coast tours, 1979-1992
Pam Windo and The Shades, Woodstock, NYC, LA, 1980-1982
Psychedelic Furs, New York, Connecticut, and US tour, 1982
The Tubes, San Francisco, guest appearances, 1984-1987
Eddie Murphy, gig, New York, 1985
Saturday Night Live, backing Todd Rundgren, 1985
Baltimore TV show, 1985
Gary Windo Band, Bottom Line, Knitting Factory, NYC, Albany, 1985-1990
Todd Rundgren's A Cappella Orchestra, Beacon Theater, NY, & US tour, 1985
The Tubes, West Coast, 198601987
Test Tube Babies, West Coast, 1987
NRBQ, Lonestar, NYC, 1991
Junior Walker, The Bear Café, Bearsville, 1991
NRBQ, Bottom Line, Albany, 1992
NRBQ, Slim's, San Francisco, 1992

GARY'S ALBUMS WITH VARIOUS ARTISTS

Septober Energy, 1971, Centipede, RCA
Tes Esat, Paris, 1971, Alan Shorter Quartet, America Records
Brotherhood, 1972, Brotherhood of Breath, RCA Neon
Running Man, 1972, Ray Russell Quintet, RCA
1984, 1973, Hugh Hopper, CBS
Secret Asylum, 1973, Ray Russell Quintet, Black Lion
Travelling Somewhere, 1973, Brotherhood of Breath, Cuneiform
Rock Bottom, 1974, Robert Wyatt, Virgin Records
Live in Willisau, 1974, Brotherhood of Breath, Ogun Records
Ruth is Stranger than Richard, 1975, Robert Wyatt, Virgin Records
Hoppertunity Box, 1976, Hugh Hopper, Compendium
European Tour '77, 1977, Carla Bley Band, Watt Records
Musique Mecanique, 1978, Carla Bley Band, Watt, ECM
More Movies, 1979, Michael Mantler, Watt Music
About Time, 1979, Daevid Allen, Charly Records, Virgin
It, 1980, Pam Windo and The Shades, Bearsville, Warner
People, 1980, NRBQ Live at the Museum of Modern Art, NY, Red Rooster
Some People, 1980, Johnny Average Band, Bearsville Records
Fictitious Sports, 1981, Nick Mason, CBS
Labotomy, 1981, M. Frog, RCA France
Amacord Nino Rota, 1981, Nino Rota tribute, Hannibal Records
Short Back 'n' Sides, 1981, Ian Hunter, Griffin Records, Chrysalis
New Jersey, 1982, Joe Piscopo, Sony Records
Forever Now, 1982, Psychedelic Furs, CBS
That's the Way I Feel Now, 1982, Thelonious Monk tribute, A&M
Lost in the Stars, 1985, Kurt Weill tribute, A&M
Crime Story sound-track, 1987, ABC TV
The Lion for Real, 1989, Allen Ginsberg, Paris Records
Flotsam Jetsam, 1994, Robert Wyatt, Rough Trade
Bremen to Bridgewater, 2004, Brotherhood of Breath, Cuneiform
Eclipse at Dawn, 2004, Brotherhood of Breath, Cuneiform

GARY'S SOLO ALBUMS

Is Vinyl Loaded, 1979, Gary Windo Quartet, unreleased
Deep Water, 1988, Antilles, Island Records
Dogface, 1982, Europa/RCA
His Master's Bones, 1996, retrospective, Cuneiform
Anglo American, 2004, retrospective, Cuneiform
Avant Gardeners, 2007, retrospective, Reel Recordings
Steam Radio Tapes, 2013, first release, Gonzo Media

PAM'S CONCERTS

Gary Windo and Friends, Maidstone College of Art, 1975
Gary and Pam Windo Duo, Maidstone College of Art, 1975
Gary Windo Quartet, Maidstone College of Art, 1975
Gary Windo and Friends, Baltimore, 1979
Pam Windo and The Shades, various gigs, White Water Depot, Woodstock, 1980–1982
Pam Windo and The Shades, Whisky-a-go-go, LA, 1980
Pam Windo and The Shades, various gigs, Joyous Lake, Woodstock, 1980–1982
Pam Windo and The Shades, The Chance, Poughkeepsie, 1980
Pam Windo and The Shades, CBGB's, NY City, 1981
Pam Windo and The Shades, Boston, 1981
Pam Windo and The Shades, Studio 54, NY City, 1981

PAM'S DISCOGRAPHY WITH GARY WINDO

It, 1980, Bearsville/Warner
Dogface, 1982, Europa
His Master's Bones, 1996, Cuneiform
Anglo American, 2004, Cuneiform
Avant Gardeners, 2007, Reel Recordings
Steam Radio Tapes, 2013, Gonzo Media

PAM'S BOOKS

Escape to Morocco, 2000, Fodor's Travel Publications
Guide to Morocco, 2000, Fodor's Travel Publications
Guide to Morocco, Second and Third Editions, 2002, 2004, Fodor's Travel Publications
Zohra's Ladder and Other Moroccan Tales, 2004, Eye Books UK
Zohra's Ladder and Other Moroccan Tales, Second Edition, 2011, Eye Books UK
Him through Me, e-book, 2013, www.pamelawindo.com

FIRST REVIEWS

"I love, love, love the book. It is an awesome read." Knox Chandler, guitarist with Gary Windo, and with Lou Reed, Marianne Faithful, and The Psychedelic Furs.

"A courageous author reliving, and bringing to an unknown reading public, her years of tender love and heartbreaking loss. We have much to learn from brave memoirs." Ellen Kleiner, Blessingway.

"The book effortlessly captures the mood, and even more importantly, recaptures the magic of a special time - in our lives and in hers. One of the most powerful and personal rock memoirs I have ever read." Dave Thompson, author, *Roger Waters: The Man behind the Wall*, and *June 1st 1974: The Greatest Supergroup of the Seventies*.

"The book is a moving, informative and inspiring read."Aymeric Leroy, writer, Canterbury Scene, author of *Pink Floyd*, and *King Crimson*.